Originals
Clare West

classic and modern
fiction and non-fiction
in English

GEORGIAN PRESS

Georgian Press (Jersey) Limited
Pirouet House
Union Street
St Helier
Jersey JE4 8ZQ
Channel Islands

© Clare West 2004

First published by Georgian Press (Jersey) Limited 2004

ISBN 1-873630-40-9 (without key)
ISBN 1-873630-41-7 (with key)

No unauthorised photocopying

All rights reserved. No part of this book may be reproduced, stored in a retrieval system, or transmitted in any form or by any means, electronic, mechanical, photocopying, recording or otherwise, without the prior permission in writing of the publishers.

Any person who does any unauthorised act in relation to this publication may be liable to criminal prosecution and civil claims for damages.

Produced by AMR Limited

Printed in Egypt by International Printing House

Contents

Acknowledgements 4

Introduction 5

1	Chris Stewart, *Driving Over Lemons* (1999)	7
2	Alexander McCall Smith, *The No. 1 Ladies' Detective Agency* (1998)	11
3	Ernest Hemingway, *The Old Man and the Sea* (1952)	15
4	John Grisham, *The Partner* (1997)	19
5	Sue Townsend, *The Secret Diary of Adrian Mole aged 13¾* (1982)	23
6	Frank McCourt, *Angela's Ashes* (1996)	29
7	Lewis Carroll, *Alice's Adventures in Wonderland* (1865)	33
8	David Hempleman-Adams, *Walking on Thin Ice* (1998)	37
9	Robert Harris, *Enigma* (1995)	41
10	Anne Tyler, *The Accidental Tourist* (1985)	45
11	Sebastian Faulks, *Birdsong* (1993)	49
12	Dodie Smith, *I Capture the Castle* (1949)	53
13	J.R.R. Tolkien, *The Fellowship of the Ring* (1954)	57
14	Graham Greene, *Our Man in Havana* (1958)	61
15	Laurie Lee, *Cider with Rosie* (1959)	65
16	Murray Bail, *Camouflage* (2000)	69
17	Susan Hill, *The Woman in Black* (1983)	73
18	John le Carré, *A Perfect Spy* (1986)	77
19	W. Somerset Maugham, *The Colonel's Lady* (1951)	81
20	Patricia Highsmith, *The Talented Mr Ripley* (1956)	85
21	Louis de Bernières, *Captain Corelli's Mandolin* (1994)	91
22	Catherine Chidgey, *Golden Deeds* (2000)	95
23	Harper Lee, *To Kill a Mockingbird* (1960)	101
24	Diana Souhami, *Selkirk's Island* (2001)	105
25	Ben Okri, *The Famished Road* (1991)	111
26	Anita Desai, *Studies in the Park* (1978)	115
27	John Steinbeck, *The Pearl* (1948)	119
28	Kazuo Ishiguro, *The Remains of the Day* (1989)	123

Index to Exercises 127

The Key begins on page 129 of the With Key edition.

Acknowledgements

The author and publishers are grateful for permission to reproduce extracts from the following copyright material:

The Accidental Tourist by Anne Tyler published by Chatto & Windus. Used by permission of The Random House Group Limited.

Angela's Ashes by Frank McCourt. Copyright © Frank McCourt 1996. Reprinted by permission of HarperCollins Publishers Limited.

Birdsong by Sebastian Faulks published by Hutchinson. Used by permission of The Random House Group Limited.

Camouflage by Murray Bail published by Harvill Press. Used by permission of The Random House Group Limited.

Captain Corelli's Mandolin by Louis de Bernières published by Vintage (May 1995). Used by permission of The Random House Group Limited.

Cider with Rosie by Laurie Lee published by Hogarth Press. Used by permission of The Random House Group Limited.

'The Colonel's Lady' from Volume II of *The Collected Short Stories* by W. Somerset Maugham published by William Heinemann. Used by permission of The Random House Group Limited.

Driving Over Lemons by Chris Stewart. Reproduced by permission of Sort Of Books.

Enigma by Robert Harris published by Hutchinson. Used by permission of The Random House Group.

The Famished Road by Ben Okri published by Orion. Copyright © Ben Okri 1991. Reproduced by permission of the author.

The Fellowship of the Ring by J.R.R. Tolkien. Copyright © The Trustees of the J.R.R. Tolkien 1967 Settlement 1954, 1966. Reprinted by permission of HarperCollins Publishers Limited.

Golden Deeds by Catherine Chidgey. By permission of Macmillan Publishers Limited, London, UK.

I Capture the Castle by Dodie Smith published by Bodley Head/Red Fox. Used by permission of The Random House Group Limited and Laurence Fitch Limited.

The No. 1 Ladies' Detective Agency by Alexander McCall Smith published by Polygon. Reproduced by permission of Birlinn Limited.

The Old Man and the Sea by Ernest Hemingway published by Jonathan Cape. Used by permission of The Random House Group Limited.

Our Man in Havana by Graham Greene published by William Heinemann. Reproduced by permission of David Higham Associates.

The Partner by John Grisham published by Century. Used by permission of The Random House Group Limited.

The Pearl by John Steinbeck (pages 69–71). Copyright © John Steinbeck 1945. Reproduced by permission of Penguin Books Limited.

A Perfect Spy by John le Carré published by Hodder. Reproduced by permission of David Higham Associates.

The Remains of the Day by Kazuo Ishiguro. Copyright © 1989 Kazuo Ishiguro. Reproduced by permission of Faber and Faber Limited and of the author c/o Rogers, Coleridge & White Limited, 20 Powis Mews, London W11 1JN.

The Secret Diary of Adrian Mole aged $13\tfrac{3}{4}$ by Sue Townsend. Used by permission of The Random House Group Limited.

Selkirk's Island by Diana Souhami published by Weidenfeld & Nicolson. Reproduced by permission of The Orion Publishing Group Limited.

'Studies in the Park' from *Games at Twilight and Other Stories* by Anita Desai. Copyright © Anita Desai 1978. Reproduced by permission of Rodgers, Coleridge & White Limited, 20 Powis Mews, London W11 1JN.

The Talented Mr Ripley by Patricia Highsmith published by William Heinemann. Used by permission of The Random House Group Limited.

To Kill a Mockingbird by Harper Lee published by William Heinemann. Used by permission of The Random House Group Limited.

Walking on Thin Ice by David Hempleman-Adams. By permission of The Orion Publishing Group Limited.

The Woman in Black by Susan Hill published by Vintage. Copyright © Susan Hill 1983. Reproduced by permission of Sheil Land Associates Limited.

Photographs by permission of: Associated Press (pages 53, 101), Faber and Faber (page 123 © Jane Brown), Hodder & Stoughton (page 77 © Jane Brown), New Zealand Book Council website, www.bookcouncil.org.nz (page 95), The Orion Publishing Group Limited (pages 37, 105, 111), Sort Of Books (page 7 © Mark Ellingham), The Random House Group Limited (pages 19 © Sam Abell, 41 © Sally Soames, 45 © Diane Walker, 49 © Jerry Bauer, 69 © Anthony Browell, 73), Rex Features (pages 11, 15, 23, 29, 33, 57, 61, 65, 81, 85, 91, 115, 119).

Cover design by Vasso Varvaki.

INTRODUCTION

Originals contains 28 extracts from classic and modern fiction and non-fiction written in English. These span well over a hundred years of writing, from Lewis Carroll's *Alice's Adventures in Wonderland*, published in 1865, to Diana Souhami's *Selkirk's Island*, published in 2001. There are extracts from classic novels and short stories, spy stories, a ghost story, thrillers, war novels, fantasy novels, novels about childhood, a biography, and contemporary fiction. The authors of these works come from many parts of the world, including India, Nigeria, Japan, New Zealand, Australia and the USA. Many of them are highly regarded in the world of literature, and have won awards for their writing. A number of the works included in *Originals* have been filmed.

The purpose of *Originals* is to encourage students to read, and to improve their English by reading. These days it is easy to pick up a magazine or switch on the television, and to miss out altogether on the great thrill of reading a well-written story or true account. Some of the best books can be quite difficult to understand, but the effort is well worth it. There's nothing like the feeling of being part of the world created by the author, surrounded by characters you become familiar with, and anxious to know what happens to them in the end.

The texts

As the title implies, these are unsimplified. They have been carefully selected for level, so that intermediate students, or those preparing for the Cambridge Preliminary English Test (PET), will be able to understand them, with the help of the notes and exercises. The devices ... or ..... are used to indicate where a few words or lines have been cut from the text.

The extracts are presented in approximate order of difficulty, starting with the easiest units. This grading should help students to gain confidence in reading as they progress through the book, so it is recommended that this order is followed.

In some units (5, 20, 22 and 24) there are two texts from the same book. They should be read in the same lesson, if possible.

Details about the authors

Each unit starts with a brief description of the author's life, and offers suggestions for further reading. There follows an introduction to the text and a *Before you read* section. Careful reading of this page, and the text itself, could be done as homework to prepare for the lesson.

Notes

The notes immediately following the text are intended to explain difficult vocabulary, structures or usage, in language suitable for the reader's level. Any ungrammatical, old-fashioned or foreign expressions are always commented on here or in the next section. Only the meaning of the word or expression as it is used in the text is given.

Working with the text

This section includes a wide variety of exercises designed to check understanding, to encourage students to reread the text, and to help them to get as much as possible out of it. Every unit has a *Reading between the lines* exercise, to get beneath the surface of the text and explore what the characters are thinking, or what the author is implying rather than stating. There is also *Discussion*, where students have a chance to talk about wider issues raised by the texts, and *Prediction*, which helps to motivate the reader to read on.

Language work

This section of the unit has two aims: to draw the reader's attention to important areas of grammar and vocabulary in the text, and to give extended practice in using them. These areas have been selected for their relevance to PET preparation, and tie in with the PET syllabus. The example word, phrase or sentence which begins each exercise always comes directly from the text. Few specific structural rules are given; students are advised to consult a suitable grammar book if they are in doubt.

Introduction

Role play

Many units have a role play which is designed to reflect the topic of the unit. It offers an opportunity for students to practise some of the language they have studied, in a dynamic, interactive way. It also looks at one aspect of the reading text from a contemporary angle.

Writing

Many units have a writing task which can be done in class or for homework. All the tasks offer practice in writing for PET; some of them adhere closely to the PET syllabus, while others include a more imaginative, creative element. Teachers are advised to consult the *PET Handbook* (available from Cambridge ESOL) for up-to-date guidelines and word limits.

Index

Teachers and students can refer to the Index on page 127 to check where a particular structure or other language area is dealt with.

A **With Key** edition of *Originals* is available.

I hope there is something to interest everybody in this selection of texts, and I wish you all good reading.

Clare West

This book is dedicated to my mother, Sybil Williams.

CHRIS STEWART
1950–

Chris Stewart was born in Sussex, England. He was the drummer in a pop group, *The Garden Wall*, which was formed by some of his school friends. This group did not last long, however, and soon Chris was invited by his friend Peter Gabriel to join another group, called *Genesis*. After *Genesis* had released two singles, *Silent Sun* and *A Winter's Tale*, Chris had to leave when the band became professional, because his parents refused to let him leave school. *Genesis* went on to become very successful. Chris left school a year later, and played drums for a circus. Soon he became interested in farming; he worked on a farm for a while, and then started a career as a travelling sheep-shearer. He also contributed to several travel books, *The Rough Guide to Andalucia* and *The Rough Guide to China*. In 1988 he bought a run-down old farm in the Alpujarras, the foothills to the south of the Sierra Nevada mountain range in Spain. He still lives there with his wife Ana and their daughter Chloë. *Driving Over Lemons* was published in 1999.

Other works by Chris Stewart: *A Parrot in a Pepper Tree*.

Driving Over Lemons

Chris Stewart has come to southern Spain to look at houses for sale in the mountains. He and his wife Ana want to live and farm there. An estate agent takes him to see a small farm, and they have lunch there with the Spanish owner. Chris has enthusiastically agreed to buy the farm and has even paid a deposit! Now he hopes that Ana won't think he has made a mistake. She is flying out from England to join him.

Before you read

1 Why do you think the book has this title? Choose **a**, **b**, or **c**. Driving over lemons ...

    a is a well-known sport in this part of Spain.
    b is hard to avoid on some Spanish roads.
    c is the best way of producing lemon juice.

2 Why do you think Chris and Ana want to move from England to Spain? Tick (✔) as many as you like.

    a They want to enjoy better weather.
    b They want to experience a different lifestyle.
    c They want to farm in the traditional Spanish way.
    d Farms are cheaper to buy in Spain than in England.

Now read to the end of the text.

Think about these questions as you read. Is the text ...

... exciting?   ... funny?   ... difficult?   ... scary?   ... sad?   ... interesting?

I collected Ana from the airport, skimming back towards Granada in the biscuit tin of a car that I had hired. We watched as the snowy peaks of the Sierra Nevada appeared from a blue haze above the city and the winter sun set the tops glowing rose pink with the last rays of the day. Ana was enchanted and I too felt a bit dazed by the beauty of it all. What a place to come and live! We left Granada behind and climbed over the pass of Suspiro del Moro. ...

Pedro and Maria had invited us to stay the night and late in the evening we turned into the valley for Ana's first view of our new home. In the light of the setting sun the fields along the road seemed even more beautiful than I had imagined. Ana seemed pleased with it all and I pointed things out to her proudly as we passed. Olives, oranges, lemons ... cabbages ... potatoes ...

We climbed up over the cliffs of the gorge and into the valley.

'There it is!'

You get a brief glimpse of El Valero just as you enter the valley, before it disappears again behind a great curtain of rock.

'Where?'

'Over there, you see? Up on the rock over the other side of the river.'

'That?'

'What do you mean "that"?'

'Precisely that – that.'

'Well "that" is it. El Valero. What do you think?'

'I don't think at all from this distance. I'll reserve judgement till we get a little nearer.'

We drove on into the valley and stopped at a nearer vantage point. 'Well, I think it really looks rather nice.'

I looked at Ana in amazement and delight. She is not generally given to such outbursts of enthusiasm.

We drove on a bit and parked the car where the road ran out. .....

The light was failing and I knew there was a long and rather tricky walk across the valley to get to the farm. We set off along the path down the hill, navigating a patch of bog where the way forded a stream, and then through a thicket of huge eucalyptus, sweet-smelling and whispering in the evening breeze, and ringing with birdsong. We emerged on the bank of the river. It tumbled full and clear down a steep bed of stones, crashing and roaring over the falls of smooth rocks and gliding in and out of the stiller pools.

I smiled and squeezed Ana's hand as we set out eagerly across the pack-bridge, excited at the prospect of our first view together of our new home.

Notes

[Some of the words and expressions are dealt with in *Working with the text*.]

skimming (line 1): (here) driving quickly
Granada (line 1): the capital city of the province
peaks (line 2): tops of the mountains
haze (line 3): mist, not a clear sky
pass (line 6): a way through the mountains
Pedro and Maria (line 7): the previous farmer and his wife
gorge (line 12): deep river valley with high sides
El Valero (line 14): the name of the farm

vantage point (line 24): a place which offers a good view
The light was failing (line 29): it was becoming dark
a patch of bog (line 30): some very wet land, unsafe to walk on
the way forded a stream (line 31): you had to walk through a stream
thicket (line 31): group of trees
eucalyptus (line 31): attractive tree, originally found in Australia
breeze (line 32): light wind
pack-bridge (line 36): narrow stone bridge, not suitable for cars

Working with the text

Do you like the text? Why or why not?

A The words and phrases on the left (1–10) are from the text. Find them, then match them with their approximate meanings (a–j).

1 enchanted
2 dazed
3 glimpse
4 disappears
5 precisely
6 reserve judgement
7 amazement
8 tricky
9 navigating
10 emerged

a exactly
b becomes impossible to see
c finding a way through
d make my mind up later
e difficult
f a quick look
g unable to think clearly
h delighted
i came out
j great surprise

B Answer the questions.

1 Where are Chris and Ana going to spend the night?
2 What do Chris and Ana find so beautiful about the views (lines 8–11)?
3 Who says, 'There it is!' and what does 'it' refer to?
4 Why do Chris and Ana have to walk some of the way to the farmhouse?
5 What is Chris a little worried about, as it is getting dark?
6 How do Chris and Ana feel, as they come closer to their new home?

C True or false? Tick (✔) any true sentences and rewrite the false ones.

1 The Sierra Nevada mountains are near Granada.
2 Ana has seen the farm before.
3 The cabbages and potatoes belong to Chris.
4 The farm can be seen all the way along the road.
5 Ana is generally an enthusiastic person.
6 Chris and Ana arrive at their new home in the evening.

D Reading between the lines

1 What does Chris mean by 'the biscuit tin of a car' (line 1)? How do you think he feels about the car?
2 Why is Chris proud of the things he points out to Ana on the way?
3 How does Chris feel about showing the farm to Ana? How do you know?
4 Why does Chris call Ana's comment 'Well, I think it really looks rather nice' (line 24) an outburst of enthusiasm?

E Match the adjectives in the first line to the nouns in the second line, to make pairs of words from the last two paragraphs. Try to do it from memory, then check with the text.

- tricky, huge, evening, steep, new
- eucalyptus, bed, home, walk, breeze

Driving Over Lemons

F Chris and Ana have to walk part of the way to El Valero. Put these sentences describing their walk in the correct order. Try to do it from memory, then check with the text.

  a They crossed a narrow bridge.
  b They passed through a group of large trees.
  c They walked through a stream.
  d They took a path going downhill.
  e They saw a fast-flowing river.

G Discussion

  1 Do you think Chris was wrong to buy the farm, when Ana hadn't seen it? How would *you* feel in her situation?
  2 Do you think Chris and Ana are crazy to make such a change in their lifestyle, or do you admire them for being so adventurous? What problems will they face, when living in a foreign country?

H Prediction

What do you think happens when they move permanently to El Valero? Tick (✔) as many as you like.

  a They stay there, and their farm brings in a lot of money.
  b They miss their friends and family and decide to return to England.
  c They just manage to make enough money to stay on their farm.
  d Chris writes a book which becomes a best-seller!
  e They have a child, and are very happy there.
  f Ana doesn't like the farm as much as Chris does.

Language work

A 'We ... stopped at a nearer vantage point' (line 24). *Nearer* is the comparative form of the adjective *near*. We add *-er* to most short adjectives, but with longer ones, we use *more*. Complete the sentences about the text with the correct form of the adjective in brackets.

  1 The countryside looked _____ than Chris had imagined. (beautiful)
  2 Ana seemed _____ than usual. (enthusiastic)
  3 Perhaps she thought El Valero was _____ than she had expected. (nice)
  4 But the distance from the road to El Valero was _____ than Chris had told her. (long)

Make three of your own comparative sentences, comparing television programmes, books, films, CDs or DVDs.

B 'Where?' 'Over there, you see?' (lines 16–17). *Where* is a question-word. Complete the questions about the text with the correct question-word from the box, and then answer the questions.

Who	Where	What

  1 ___ colour are the mountain peaks?
  2 ___ is Suspiro del Moro?
  3 ___ are the farm's previous owners?
  4 ___ kinds of fruit are growing along the road?
  5 ___ do Chris and Ana park the car?
  6 ___ exactly are the birds singing?

Now think of three questions you would like to ask Chris Stewart about his move from England to El Valero.

Writing

Imagine you are Ana. Write a postcard (35–45 words) to a friend in England, a few days after your arrival in Spain. In your card, you should:

- say what you like about the farm
- say what you don't like about the farm
- invite your friend to come and stay.

ALEXANDER McCALL SMITH
1948–

Alexander McCall Smith, known as Sandy to his friends, was born in Zimbabwe and educated there and in Scotland. He is Professor of Medical Law at the University of Edinburgh. He has lectured at various universities in Africa, including in Botswana, where he lived for a time. As well as writing books on medical law, criminal law and philosophy, he has also written children's books, collections of short stories and novels. *The No. 1 Ladies' Detective Agency* (1998) received two Booker Judges' Special Recommendations. Alexander McCall Smith was named Author of the Year in the British National Book Awards 2004.

Alexander McCall Smith is married to a doctor and has two daughters. He lives in Edinburgh, Scotland.

Other works by Alexander McCall Smith: *Tears of the Giraffe, Morality for Beautiful Girls, The Kalahari Typing School for Men, The Full Cupboard of Life*.

The No. 1 Ladies' Detective Agency

The story is set in Botswana, southern Africa. When Precious Ramotswe's father dies, his last wish is for Precious to have her own business. And so, with the money from selling her father's cattle, Precious sets up a detective agency in an office overlooking the Kalahari Desert.

One of the first people to ask her for help is a young woman called Happy Bapetsi. Happy is single, with a good job and her own house. Her problem is that a man has turned up, saying he is her father. She doesn't recognise him, because her father left the family a long time ago. She has taken him into her house and pays for everything he needs, but she wants to find out if he is really her father. Precious thinks of a plan, and drives to Happy's house while Happy is at work.

Before you read

1 Why do you think the book is called *The No. 1 Ladies' Detective Agency*? Choose **a**, **b**, **c** or **d**.

   a It's the best detective agency in the world.
   b It's the first of three agencies in Botswana, Zimbabwe and Zambia.
   c Precious is the most important lady in Gaborone, capital of Botswana.
   d It's the only detective agency in Botswana run by a lady.

2 *Precious* means very valuable. Why do you think Precious's parents gave her this name?

3 How do you think Precious will find out if the man is Happy's father or not? Choose **a**, **b**, **c** or **d**. She will ...

   a look at his birth certificate.
   b ask Happy's mother to identify him.
   c persuade him to admit he isn't Happy's father.
   d persuade him to take a blood test.

Now read to the end of the text.

Think about these questions as you read. Is the text ...

... exciting?   ... funny?   ... difficult?   ... scary?   ... sad?   ... interesting?

As Precious neared the house, she increased her speed. This was an errand of mercy, after all, and if the Daddy were sitting in his chair outside the front door he would have to see her arrive in a cloud of dust. The Daddy was there, of course, enjoying the morning sun, and he sat up straight in his chair as he saw the tiny white van sweep up to the gate. Mma Ramotswe turned off the engine and ran out of the car up to the house.

'Dumela Rra,' she greeted him rapidly. 'Are you Happy Bapetsi's Daddy?'

The Daddy rose to his feet. 'Yes,' he said proudly. 'I am the Daddy.'

Mma Ramotswe panted, as if trying to get her breath back.

'I'm sorry to say that there has been an accident. Happy was run over and is very sick at the hospital. Even now they are performing a big operation on her.'

The Daddy let out a wail. 'Aiee! My daughter! My little baby Happy!'

A good actor, thought Mma Ramotswe, unless... No, she preferred to trust Happy Bapetsi's instinct. A girl should know her own Daddy even if she had not seen him since she was a baby.

'Yes,' she went on. 'It is very sad. She is very sick, very sick. And they need lots of blood to make up for all the blood she's lost.'

The Daddy frowned. 'They must give her that blood. Lots of blood. I can pay.'

'It's not the money,' said Mma Ramotswe. 'Blood is free. We don't have the right sort. We will have to get some from her family, and you are the only one she has. We must ask you for some blood.'

The Daddy sat down heavily.

'I'm an old man,' he said.

Mme Ramotswe sensed that it would work. Yes, this man was an impostor.

'That is why we are asking you,' she said. 'Because she needs so much blood, they will have to take about half your blood. And that is very dangerous for you. In fact, you might die.'

The Daddy's mouth fell open.

'Die?'

'Yes,' said Mma Ramotswe. 'But then you are her father and we know that you would do this thing for your daughter. Now could you come quickly, or it will be too late. Doctor Moghile is waiting.'

The Daddy opened his mouth, and then closed it.

'Come on,' said Mma Ramotswe, reaching down and taking his wrist. 'I'll help you to the van.'

The Daddy rose to his feet, and then tried to sit down again. Mma Ramotswe gave him a tug.

'No,' he said, 'I don't want to.'

'You must,' said Mma Ramotswe. 'Now come on.'

The Daddy shook his head. 'No,' he said faintly. 'I won't.'

Notes
increased her speed (line 1): drove faster
errand of mercy (line 1): (here) doing something to save a life
the Daddy (line 2): the man who calls himself Happy's father
tiny (line 4): very small
van (line 5) a kind of car for carrying goods
sweep up (line 5): (here) drive fast
Mma (line 5): (Setswana) used when speaking to a woman (Mma rhymes with *ah*)
Dumela Rra (line 7): (Setswana) a polite greeting for a man (Rra rhymes with *ah*)
panted (line 9): breathed in and out very quickly

run over (line 10): knocked down by a car
let out a wail. 'Aiee!' (line 12): gave a loud, sad cry
instinct (line 14): something a person knows without being told
frowned (line 18): brought his eyebrows together, looked worried or angry
sensed (line 24): had a feeling
impostor (line 24): someone pretending to be another person
wrist (line 34): the joint between the hand and the arm
gave him a tug (line 36): pulled him suddenly
faintly (line 40): very quietly and weakly

Working with the text

Do you like the text? Why or why not?

A Answer the questions.
1 Where is 'the Daddy' when Precious Ramotswe arrives?
2 What does the man do when Precious tells him that Happy has had an accident?
3 Does Precious believe him?
4 What does the man offer to do when he hears that Happy needs blood?

B Reading between the lines
1 Why does Precious call her visit to Happy's house 'an errand of mercy' (line 1)?
2 Why do you think the man is sitting in the sun and not working?
3 Why do you think the man is proud and pleased to be Happy's father?
4 Why does Precious pretend to be out of breath?
5 Why doesn't Precious believe that this man is Happy's real father?
6 How does Precious prove that the man is an impostor?

C The verbs on the left (1–8) come from the text. Match them with their objects (a–h). Try to do it from memory, then check with the text.

1	increased	a	her breath back
2	enjoying	b	the engine
3	turned off	c	his wrist
4	get	d	the right sort
5	performing	e	her speed
6	don't have	f	his mouth
7	opened	g	the morning sun
8	taking	h	a big operation

D What exactly is Precious's plan? Put the sentences in the correct order.
a She offers to take Happy's father to the hospital in her van.
b She points out that Happy's father will have to give a lot of blood, and could die.
c When the man refuses, Precious knows he isn't really Happy's father.
d Precious rushes off to Happy's house.
e She explains that Happy is badly hurt and needs her father's blood.
f She tells 'the Daddy' there has been an accident.

E Discussion
1 What do you think of Precious's plan? Can you think of a better one?
2 What would *you* do if someone arrived at your house, saying he was your long-lost brother or cousin? Can you think of a way of finding out if he really was one of your family?
3 Do you think young people should take care of their parents, as they do in Botswana?

F Prediction

What do you think happens next? Tick (✔) as many as you like.

a The man pretends he is too ill to give blood.
b The man admits he is not Happy's father.
c Precious is very angry with him.
d Happy is sorry for him and decides to let him stay in her house.
e The man returns to his home town, and Happy is happy again.

Language work

A 'A good actor, thought Mma Ramotswe, unless...' (line 13). *Unless* here really means *but perhaps*. The missing words are probably 'he is telling the truth.' Precious Ramotswe is thinking, 'What a good actor! But perhaps he is telling the truth.' Match these parts of sentences, which are all linked with *unless* used in this way.

1 Tricia looks rather sad,
2 There's something wrong with the car,
3 I think they went to Austria,
4 Steve seems very happy,
5 I think that's my aunt over there,

a unless it's just running out of petrol.
b unless it was Australia!
c unless it's someone who looks like her.
d unless she's just thinking about something.
e unless he's just pretending.

B 'In fact, you might die' (line 26). *Might* is a modal verb used to show that something is possible. Complete each sentence with *might* and one of the words or phrases from the box.

see	come	hurt	get
catch cold		damage it	

1 I'm not lending you my car. You're a terrible driver – you _____!
2 Don't go out now – it's freezing! You _____!
3 I _____ to the football match on Saturday, but I'm not sure yet. Will you all be there?
4 Don't try and lift that snooker table. It's really heavy. You _____ your back.
5 My brother _____ a place at college. It all depends on his exam results.
6 I _____ you at the meeting – I'm not sure if I'll be there or not.

Now make two of your own sentences with *might*.

C '... an errand of mercy' (line 1), '... a cloud of dust' (line 3). *A/an* is the indefinite article. We use *an* in front of words beginning with a, e, i, o, u, and h when it isn't sounded. We use *a* in front of all other letters, and also u and eu when they sound like 'you'. Complete the phrases with *a* or *an*.

1 ___ Italian jacket
2 ___ horrible place
3 ___ university teacher
4 ___ hour and ___ half
5 ___ boiled egg
6 ___ awful taste
7 ___ history book
8 ___ exciting film
9 ___ very exciting film
10 ___ unhappy life
11 ___ European country
12 ___ umbrella
13 ___ orange
14 ___ year or two
15 ___ helpful policeman

Role play

Student A: You are talking to your friend (Student B) about giving blood. You think it's an excellent idea, and you give blood to the national blood bank as often as possible. Explain to Student B how useful it could be in saving someone's life, and try to persuade him or her to go along with you next time.

Student B: You hate the thought of blood, and feel faint whenever you see any blood. You can see how useful a blood bank is. You are impressed that Student A gives blood so often, but you don't want to do it yourself! However, when Student A explains how easy it all is, perhaps you agree to give it a try.

Writing

You are a private detective, and you are investigating a problem for a client. Write an e-mail (35–45 words) to the client. In your e-mail, you should:

- describe the progress you have made
- say how much the client owes you
- ask the client to come to your office.

3 ERNEST HEMINGWAY
1899–1961

Ernest Miller Hemingway was born in Chicago, Illinois, USA. He started work as a junior reporter in Kansas. In World War I he became an ambulance driver for the Red Cross, but after the war he moved to Paris, to work for a Canadian newspaper and to write short stories. His interests were bullfighting, fishing and hunting, all of which he wrote about in his stories. During the Spanish Civil War he worked as a journalist in Spain, and used his experiences there to write *For Whom the Bell Tolls*, which many readers consider his greatest novel. In 1940 he moved to Cuba, with his second wife. He reported on World War II as a journalist travelling with American troops, and after the war he started writing fiction again. In 1953 he won the Pulitzer Prize for his 1952 short novel *The Old Man and the Sea*, and a year later he was awarded the Nobel Prize in Literature. He returned to the USA, but he began to feel ill and depressed. He killed himself with a shotgun in 1961.

Other works by Ernest Hemingway: *The Torrents of Spring, The Sun Also Rises, Men Without Women, A Farewell to Arms, Death in the Afternoon, Winner Take Nothing, The Green Hills of Africa, To Have or Have Not, For Whom the Bell Tolls, Across the River and Into the Trees, Islands in the Stream, The Garden of Eden.*

The Old Man and the Sea

This is a story about an old man called Santiago. He is a fisherman, who lives in a village near Havana in Cuba. For many weeks now he has not managed to catch a fish, and no one will sail with him, because they think he is unlucky. But the boy who used to sail with him still believes Santiago is a great fisherman, and looks after the old man whenever he can. Now Santiago is alone on the open sea in his small boat, and to his surprise he has hooked a very large fish on his fishing line. The fish is so big that it is pulling Santiago's boat through the water.

Before you read

1. Why do you think the old man has not managed to catch any fish for a long time? Choose the most likely reason (**a**, **b**, **c**, **d**, or **e**), in your opinion.

    a He has been unlucky.
    b He has forgotten all his fishing skills.
    c There have been no fish in the area.
    d He hasn't had any help from anyone.
    e He is getting too old to handle the boat and fishing lines.

2. Why do you think the old man still goes fishing? Tick (✔) as many as you like.

    a He knows no other way of passing the time.
    b He wants to show people he can still catch fish.
    c He needs to sell fish to buy enough food to live on.
    d He wants to make the boy happy, by proving that he is right.

Now read to the end of the text.

Think about these questions as you read. Is the text …

… exciting?   … funny?   … difficult?   … scary?   … sad?   … interesting?

The boat began to move slowly off toward the north-west.

The fish moved steadily and they travelled slowly on the calm water. The other baits were still in the water but there was nothing to be done.

'I wish I had the boy,' the old man said aloud.

'I'm being towed by a fish. ... I could make the line fast. But then he could break it. I must hold him all I can and give him line when he must have it. Thank God he is travelling and not going down.'

What I will do if he decides to go down, I don't know. What I'll do if he sounds and dies I don't know. But I'll do something. There are plenty of things I can do.

He held the line against his back and watched its slant in the water and the skiff moving steadily to the north-west.

This will kill him, the old man thought. He can't do this for ever. But four hours later the fish was still swimming steadily out to sea, towing the skiff, and the old man was still braced solidly with the line across his back.

'It was noon when I hooked him,' he said. 'And I have never seen him.'

He had pushed his straw hat hard down on his head before he hooked the fish and it was cutting his forehead. He was thirsty too and he got down on his knees and, being careful not to jerk on the line, moved as far into the bow as he could get and reached the water bottle with one hand. He opened it and drank a little. Then he rested against the bow. He rested sitting on the unstepped mast and sail and tried not to think but only to endure.

Then he looked behind him and saw that no land was visible. That makes no difference, he thought. I can always come in on the glow from Havana. There are two more hours before the sun sets and maybe he will come up before that. If he doesn't, maybe he will come up with the moon. If he does not do that, maybe he will come up with the sunrise. I have no cramps and I feel strong. It is he that has the hook in his mouth. But what a fish to pull like that. He must have his mouth shut tight on the wire. I wish I could see him. I wish I could see him only once to know what I have against me.

The fish never changed his course nor his direction all that night as far as the man could tell from watching the stars. It was cold after the sun went down and the old man's sweat dried cold on his back and his arms and his old legs.

ERNEST HEMINGWAY

> **Notes**
> *steadily* (line 2): at the same speed most of the time
> *baits* (line 3): pieces of food to attract fish
> *towed* (line 5): pulled along
> *make the line fast* (line 5): fix the line at a certain length
> *give him line* (line 6): let more line out for the fish
> *sounds* (line 8): dives downwards swiftly and deeply
> *slant* (line 10): angle, direction
> *skiff* (line 10): small sailing boat
> *braced* (line 14): in one position, with his muscles tight to keep himself strong and steady
> *noon* (line 15): midday
> *hooked* (line 15): caught the fish on a piece of metal at the end of a fishing line
> *jerk* (line 18): pull suddenly
> *bow* (line 18): (rhymes with *cow*) the front part of a boat
> *mast* (line 20): tall wooden or metal pole used to hold up the sail
> *unstepped* (line 20): (of the mast) lying flat on the boat, not in use
> *endure* (line 21): wait and suffer
> *glow* (line 23): (here) distant lights
> *cramps* (line 26): bad pains in hands or legs
> *wire* (line 28): fishing line
> *sweat* (line 32): salty water that comes out of your skin when you are hot

Working with the text

Do you like the text? Why or why not?

A Answer the questions.

1 Which direction is the boat travelling in?
2 Who or what is pulling the boat?
3 What time is it when the old man says, 'I have never seen him' (line 15)?
4 What is the old man wearing on his head?
5 What does the old man fetch from the bow of the boat?
6 Why is no land visible (line 22)?
7 What does 'he' refer to in 'maybe he will come up before that' (line 24)?
8 At night, how does the old man know what direction the boat is travelling in?

B Reading between the lines

1 Why do you think the old man wishes he had the boy with him?
2 What are the two things the old man is most worried about?
3 Why do you think the old man holds the fishing line 'against his back' (line 10)?
4 How do you think the old man feels about the fish? Is he confident of catching him, or frightened of dying alone at sea, or impressed by the fish's strength and size?
5 Does the old man feel tired, after drinking a little water (line 19)? How do you know?
6 Can you explain what 'I can always come in on the glow from Havana' (line 23) means? Put this sentence into your own words.
7 Why does the old man want the fish to come up out of the water?

C True or false? Tick (✔) any true sentences and rewrite the false ones.

1 The old man has several lines in the water.
2 The old man cannot see the fish.
3 The fish is swimming towards the coast.
4 The old man drinks some fruit juice.
5 The old man plans to sail into the city of Havana.
6 After the sun goes down, it is a warm night.

D Discussion

1 What are the dangers of this fishing trip for the old man? If it is so dangerous, why does he do it? Would *you* feel confident, alone on the ocean like this? What dangerous activities, if any, do *you* do?
2 How do you feel about fishing and other kinds of hunting and killing wild animals? Is it acceptable if the fishermen and hunters need to kill the animals for food? Or should people never kill wild animals for any reason?

E Prediction

What do you think happens next? Choose **a**, **b**, **c** or **d** to complete the sentences.

1 The fish **a** is brought home by the old man. **b** manages to escape. **c** causes the old man's death. **d** is completely eaten by other fish.
2 The old man **a** falls into the sea and dies. **b** sails back to his village. **c** only sees the fish once. **d** never wants to go fishing again.
3 The boy **a** loses interest in the old man. **b** sails with the old man next time. **c** sells the fish for a lot of money. **d** goes to live in Havana.

The Old Man and the Sea

Language work

A 'If he doesn't, maybe he will come up with the moon' (line 24). This is an example of the first conditional. Match these parts of sentences to make first conditional sentences. Use each item only once.

1. If I can get a cheap ticket,
2. If Joe feels well enough,
3. If we don't see you at the station,
4. I won't tell anyone
5. Sharon won't be able to help
6. The police will tow away your car

a if you don't want me to.
b if you park it there!
c he'll be at work tomorrow.
d if you don't ask her!
e we'll meet up at the hotel.
f I'll fly to Sydney.

Now make two first conditional sentences about yourself or your friends.

B 'But four hours later the fish was still swimming steadily out to sea' (line 12). *Was swimming* is an example of the past continuous, describing what the fish was doing over a long time. Complete the following sentences, putting the verbs in brackets into the past continuous.

1. It (rain) quite hard while we (shop) this morning.
2. Natalie (talk) all the time I (try) to do my homework.
3. The guards (not listen) to the prisoners, who (plan) their escape.
4. It was breakfast-time – I (drink) my coffee and (read) the newspaper.
5. (You sing) while you (have) your bath? I thought I heard you.
6. No one (listen) to the woman while she (tell) her story.
7. Two hours later I (still drive) and the boys (still sleep) in the back of the car.
8. I (not watch) TV just then – I (do) my homework!

C 'He must have his mouth shut tight on the wire' (line 27). This use of *must* shows what is probably true, although we don't know for certain. Match the statements or questions (1–6) with the most suitable answers (a–f). Use each item only once.

1. Isn't Pete at school?
2. The computer's crashed again!
3. Mum's agreed to lend me her car!
4. I can't find my mobile phone.
5. You must be Clare West?
6. It must be time for lunch by now.

a She must be mad!
b Yes, that's me.
c It must be in your pocket.
d No, he isn't. He must be ill.
e Yes, I'm really hungry.
f Oh no! There must be something wrong with it.

Think of two more sentences which use *must* in this way.

Role play

Student A: You and your friend (Student B) are planning a sailing holiday together. You're an experienced sailor and want an independent holiday, so you want to hire a small boat which you can sail round the coast, visiting any islands or villages which look interesting. You would both sleep on the boat, although there wouldn't be any space for storing clothes or cooking or washing. You're confident you'll have no difficulty in managing the boat, and look forward to being out on the open sea. Try to get your friend to agree to your plan, which would certainly be fairly cheap.

Student B: You are rather nervous about sailing, as you've only been in a boat once, and don't think you will feel safe with your friend taking charge of the boat. You would also prefer a more comfortable, luxurious holiday (you do like to wash occasionally!). So you would like to book places on a larger boat or yacht with a professional captain and crew, who would know what to do if there was a storm or other emergency. Explain your worries to Student A, and try to persuade him or her that your idea is much better.

4 JOHN GRISHAM
1955–

John Grisham was born in Jonesboro, Arkansas, USA. As a boy he had no dreams of becoming a writer, although he loved reading. He studied law at Mississippi State University, and practised both as a criminal lawyer and a civil lawyer. He entered politics and was elected to the Mississippi legislature, but resigned in 1990. He wrote his first book, *A Time to Kill*, in 1987 and had some difficulty getting it published, but it became a best-seller. His next book, *The Firm*, was so successful that he was able to build his dream house, give up his law practice, and concentrate on writing. He continued to write best-sellers, and several of his books have been made into films – *The Pelican Brief*, starring Denzel Washington and Julia Roberts, *The Chamber*, starring Chris O'Donnell and Gene Hackman, and *The Rainmaker*, with Matt Damon and Claire Danes. *The Partner* was published in 1997.

John Grisham lives with his family in Virginia and Mississippi, USA.

Other works by John Grisham: *A Time to Kill, The Firm, The Pelican Brief, The Client, The Chamber, The Rainmaker, The Runaway Jury, The Street Lawyer, The Testament, The Brethren, A Painted House, The Summons*.

The Partner

A partner in an American law firm, Patrick Lanigan, stole $90 million from the firm, pretended to die in a car crash, and escaped to Brazil. A lot of people wanted to find him – his partners, life insurance companies, the FBI. Patrick has a woman friend who is looking after the money for him. Now that Patrick has been caught and is being kept on a US base in Puerto Rico, all these people are looking for *her*. She is moving from place to place, trying to keep one step ahead of the people who are following her.

Before you read

1 If you had to hide somewhere, which country would you choose, and why?

- the Republic of Ireland
- Brazil
- the USA
- your own country
- Australia
- Fiji
- Libya
- another country

2 If you did not want anyone to recognise you, what would you change about yourself, and why?

- name
- passport
- voice
- hair
- skin colour
- clothes
- nose
- eye colour
- something else

Now read the text up to 'Why not visit her country?' (line 6).

Think about these questions as you read. Is the text …

… exciting?   … funny?   … difficult?   … scary?   … sad?   … interesting?

In Miami, she hid in an airport lounge for an hour, sipping expensive water and watching the throngs come and go. At the Varig counter, she bought a first-class ticket to São Paulo, one way. She wasn't sure why. São Paulo wasn't home, but it was certainly in the right direction. Maybe she would hide there in a nice hotel for a few days. She'd be closer to her father, wherever he was. Planes were leaving for a hundred destinations. Why not visit her country?

As it routinely does, the FBI issued an alert to customs and immigration personnel, as well as to the airlines. This one specified a young woman, age thirty-one, traveling under a Brazilian passport, real name of Eva Miranda but probably using an alias. Having learned the identity of her father, getting her real name was a simple matter. When Leah Pires walked through a passport checkpoint at Miami International, she wasn't expecting trouble in front of her. She was still looking for the men behind her.

Her Leah Pires passport had proven quite reliable in the past two weeks.

But the customs agent had seen the alert an hour earlier during a coffee break. He pushed an alarm button on his scanner while he slowly examined every word of the passport. The hesitation at first was annoying, then Leah realized something was wrong. The travelers at the other booths were breezing through, barely slowing long enough to open their passports and having the approvals nodded back at them. A supervisor in a navy jacket appeared from nowhere and huddled with the agent. 'Could you step in here, Ms Pires?' he asked politely but with no room for discussion. He was pointing at a row of doors down the wide corridor.

'Is there a problem?' she insisted.

'Not really. Just a few questions.' He was waiting for her. A uniformed guard with Mace and a gun on his waist was waiting too. The supervisor was holding her passport. Dozens of passengers behind her were watching.

'Questions about what?' she demanded as she walked with the supervisor and the guard to the second door.

'Just a few questions,' he repeated, opening the door and escorting her into a square room with no windows. A holding room. She noticed the name of Rivera on his lapel. He didn't look to be Hispanic.

'Give me the passport,' she demanded as soon as they were alone and the door was closed.

'Not so fast, Ms Pires. I need to ask you a few questions.'

'And I don't have to answer them.'

'Please, relax. Have a seat. Can I get you some coffee or water?'

'No.'

'Is this a valid address in Rio?'

'It certainly is.'

'Where did you arrive from?'

'Pensacola.'

'Your flight?'

'Airlink 855.'

'And your destination?'

'São Paulo.'

JOHN GRISHAM

Notes
sipping (line 1): drinking a little at a time
throngs (line 2): crowds of people
Varig (line 2): the national airline of Brazil
São Paulo (line 3): the largest city in Brazil
FBI (line 7): Federal Bureau of Investigation
alert (line 7): a call to watch out for someone
personnel (line 7): staff
alias (line 9): false name
scanner (line 15): (here) machine which checks passports
travelers (line 17) (American spelling): travellers (British spelling)
booths (line 17): (here) customs checkpoints
breezing through (line 17): going quickly through

barely (line 17): hardly
supervisor (line 19): senior officer
navy (line 19): dark blue colour
huddled with (line 19): (American) had a whispered conversation with
Mace (line 24): spray causing tears and sickness, used by US police and guards
dozens (line 25): large number (a dozen = 12)
escorting her (line 28): taking her
lapel (line 29): part of his jacket, where he is wearing a name badge
Hispanic (line 30): (here) Latin American
valid (line 37): genuine, real

Working with the text

A Match the adjectives (1–4) to the nouns (a–d), to make pairs of words from the text. Try to do it from memory, then check with the text.

1 expensive   a hotel
2 first-class   b ticket
3 right   c water
4 nice   d direction

B There are mistakes in all these sentences. Find them and correct them.

1 The woman hides in a Miami hotel for two hours.
2 She drinks expensive champagne.
3 She buys a one-way ticket to Paris.
4 Her home is in São Paulo.
5 She wants to be closer to her mother.

C Reading between the lines

1 Which country do you think she comes from?
2 Does she know exactly where her father is? How do you know?

D Prediction

What do you think happens in the next part of the text? Tick (✔) as many as you like. Does she …

a get caught?
b arrive in São Paulo?
c find her father?
d stay in Miami?

Now read to the end of the text.

Do you like the text? Why or why not?

E Answer the questions.

1 Which groups of people does the FBI send out an alert to?
2 Why is it easy for the FBI to find out the woman's real name?
3 Why isn't she expecting trouble at the customs booth?
4 How does the customs agent call for help?
5 When does the woman realise something is wrong?
6 Why does she agree to go into the 'holding room'?

F The words and phrases on the left (1–6) are from the text. Find them, then match them with their approximate meanings (a–f).

1 traveling under   a convinced everybody
2 a simple matter   b the place you are
3 proven quite reliable   going to
4 with no room for   c an easy thing to do
  discussion   d appear to be
5 look to be   e using
6 your destination   f firmly

G Reading between the lines

1 Why is the woman surprised to see the supervisor's name?
2 What is her attitude during the interview?
3 Do you think she is really Eva Miranda or Leah Pires?

The Partner

H Discussion

1 If you were stopped and interviewed by customs officers, would you try to be more polite, relaxed and helpful than the woman? Or would you be angry and indignant, like her?
2 The customs officer can easily prove she is lying. Did she prepare her story well enough?
3 Is it always better to tell the truth to the police and customs officers, or was she right to tell lies? What would you do, in her situation?

I Prediction

What do you think happens next? Tick (✔) as many as you like.

a The customs officer finds out who the woman really is.
b Patrick is allowed to go free.
c The woman escapes to a different country and spends all Patrick's money.
d Patrick is sent to prison for life.
e The woman is kidnapped by Patrick's partners.

Language work

A '... I don't have to answer them' (line 34). *Don't have to* is a modal verb meaning *needn't*. Complete the sentences with the correct modal verb from the box. There is one extra which you don't need.

ought	would	may	mustn't	can
	don't have to		should	

1 You _____ smoke here! It's not allowed!
2 I _____ take a day off work tomorrow. I'm not sure yet.
3 _____ you mind giving me a hand?
4 Look, I _____ do it if I don't want to.
5 Don't you think you _____ start saving some money soon?
6 I _____ come round at 7 pm, if you like.

B 'The hesitation at first was annoying' (line 16). *At first* is a phrase used as an adverb. Complete the sentences with the correct phrase from the box.

at least	at last	at night	at all	at once
at the most	at her best	at the moment		

1 The electrician's coming on Tuesday. _____, I think he said Tuesday. I could be wrong.
2 During the day the view from the apartment was nothing special, but _____ you could see the whole city lit up.
3 Hurry up. Call the police _____!

4 'What are you going to spend on your new car?' 'Oh, £1000 _____. That's all I've got!'
5 What are you doing _____? Any chance of a cup of coffee?
6 'How was your game with Angela?' 'She wasn't playing _____, so I won.'
7 It has taken me half a lifetime, but _____ I've found a dentist I like!
8 Isn't there anything _____ you'd like to eat? Not even a piece of fruit?

Choose two of these adverb phrases and put them in your own sentences.

C 'Give me the passport' (line 31). After the verbs *give, take, send, bring, show, hand* and *pass*, we usually put the indirect object (*me*) before the direct object (*passport*). Put the words in these sentences in the correct order.

1 please the pass me salt
2 you message a can give him ?
3 I'll the by you photos e-mail send
4 you us the bring menu could possibly ?
5 show I'll the you plants could buy you
6 her handed the to documents sign lawyer the
7 when hospital visited I I took flowers her in some her

Writing

Your English teacher has asked you to write a story (about 100 words). Your story must have the following title:

An exciting afternoon at the airport

5 SUE TOWNSEND
1946–

Sue Townsend was born in Leicester, England. She left school at fifteen and had a number of unskilled jobs. By her 18th birthday she was married, and a year later had her first baby. In 1978 she joined a writers' group and her career as an author started from there. Her first play, *Womberang*, won a Thames Television award. Since then she has written several stage plays and adapted one of her novels for the stage. She is best known, however, for writing *The Secret Diary of Adrian Mole aged 13¾* (published in 1982) and its follow-up, *The Growing Pains of Adrian Mole*, which were both number-one best-sellers, making Sue Townsend the best-selling novelist of the 1980s. The Adrian Mole diaries have sold over 8 million copies, have been adapted for radio, television and theatre, and have been translated into 34 languages.

Sue Townsend is married and lives in Leicester.

Other works by Sue Townsend: *The Growing Pains of Adrian Mole, Rebuilding Coventry, Adrian Mole from Minor to Major, The Queen and I, Adrian Mole – The Wilderness Years, Ghost Children, Adrian Mole – The Cappuccino Years, Public Confessions of a Middle-aged Woman aged 55¾*.

The Secret Diary of Adrian Mole aged 13¾

Adrian Mole is a teenage boy who lives with his father and mother and the family dog. He has a lot of problems to worry about, and writes them all down in his secret diary.

Before you read

What problems do you think Adrian has? Tick (✔) as many as you like.

- **a** He thinks he isn't good-looking.
- **b** His parents tell him what to do all the time.
- **c** He is worried about his health.
- **d** His teachers don't like him.
- **e** He hasn't got a girlfriend.

Now read the first text.

Think about these questions as you read. Is the text …

… exciting?   … funny?   … difficult?   … scary?   … sad?   … interesting?

Thursday January 1st
BANK HOLIDAY IN ENGLAND, IRELAND, SCOTLAND AND WALES
These are my New Year's resolutions:
1. I will help the blind across the road.
2. I will hang my trousers up.
3. I will put the sleeves back on my records.
4. I will not start smoking.
5. I will stop squeezing my spots.
6. I will be kind to the dog.
7. I will help the poor and ignorant.

• • • • •

Eight days have gone by since Christmas Day but my mother still hasn't worn the green lurex apron I bought her for Christmas! She will get bathcubes next year.

Just my luck, I've got a spot on my chin for the first day of the New Year!

Saturday January 3rd
I shall go mad through lack of sleep! My father has banned the dog from the house so it barked outside my window all night. Just my luck!

• • • • •

I think the spot is a boil. Just my luck to have it where everybody can see it. I pointed out to my mother that I hadn't had any vitamin C today. She said, 'Go and buy an orange, then'. This is typical.

She still hasn't worn the lurex apron.

I will be glad to get back to school.

Sunday January 4th
My father has got the flu. I'm not surprised with the diet we get. My mother went out in the rain to get him a vitamin C drink, but as I told her, 'It's too late now'. It's a miracle we don't get scurvy. My mother says she can't see anything on my chin, but this is guilt because of the diet.

The dog has run off because my mother didn't close the gate. I have broken the arm on the stereo. Nobody knows yet, and with a bit of luck my father will be ill for a long time. He is the only one who uses it apart from me. No sign of the apron.

SUE TOWNSEND

> **Notes**
> *Bank Holiday* (line 2): public holiday
> *New Year's resolutions* (line 3): at New Year you make promises to do things differently this year
> *the blind* (line 4): people who cannot see
> *sleeves* (line 6): covers of records or LPs
> *spots* (line 8): small red bumps on (especially a teenager's) skin
> *squeezing* (line 8): pushing (a spot) with two fingers together
> *ignorant* (line 10): people who know nothing or are not educated
> *lurex* (line 12): shiny nylon material, often used for party clothes
> *apron* (line 12): something cooks wear in the kitchen to protect their clothes
> *bathcubes* (line 12): perfumed salts for a bath
> *chin* (line 13): pointed part of your face below your mouth
> *barked* (line 16): (the dog) made a loud noise
> *boil* (line 17): infected spot
> *pointed out to* (line 18): informed
> *flu* (line 23): illness like a very bad cold with a high temperature
> *diet* (line 23): the kind of food people eat every day
> *It's a miracle* (line 25): it's really surprising
> *scurvy* (line 25): illness sailors used to get because they didn't eat enough fresh fruit and vegetables
> *guilt* (line 26): the feeling that something is your fault
> *arm on the stereo* (line 27): (on an old-fashioned record-player) this holds the needle and puts it down on the record or LP to make it play

Working with the text

Do you like the first text? Why or why not?

A Answer the questions.

1 What has Adrian given his mother as a Christmas present?
2 Why didn't Adrian sleep well on Friday night?
3 Why is Adrian worried about the spot on his chin?
4 What does Adrian think is the reason for his father's flu?
5 Why does the dog run away?
6 What is wrong with the stereo?

B The verbs on the left (1–8) are from the first text. Match them with their objects (a–h). Try to do it from memory, then check with the text.

1	help	a	the dog
2	hang	b	the green lurex apron
3	put	c	my spots
4	squeezing	d	the blind
5	worn	e	my trousers up
6	banned	f	the gate
7	buy	g	the sleeves back
8	close	h	an orange

C Reading between the lines

1 What kind of person is Adrian *before* his New Year's resolutions, do you think? Think of at least three adjectives to describe him.
2 Why does Adrian plan to give his mother bathcubes for Christmas next year?
3 Why does Adrian point out to his mother that he hasn't had any vitamin C? How does he feel about the food he is given at home? Do you think his mother feels 'guilty'?
4 Why is Adrian hoping his father will be ill for a long time?
5 What are the three things which Adrian says are 'Just my luck'? What does this expression mean?

D Discussion

1 What New Year's resolutions do *you* make? Do you keep them, or do you forget them a few days later?
2 Why is Adrian so critical of his parents? Is this how all teenagers see their parents?

E Prediction

What do you think happens next? Tick (✔) as many as you like.

a Adrian continues to worry about the spot on his chin.
b Adrian falls in love.
c Adrian's mother invites their neighbours to dinner.
d Adrian gets angry with his best friend.

Now read the second text.

Wednesday January 14th

Joined the library. Got *Care of the Skin, Origin of Species,* and a book by a woman my mother is always going on about. It is called *Pride and Prejudice,* by a woman called Jane Austen. I could tell the librarian was impressed. Perhaps she is an intellectual like me. She didn't look at my spot, so perhaps it is getting smaller. About time!

   Mr Lucas was in the kitchen drinking coffee with my mother. ... They were laughing, but when I went in, they stopped.

   Mrs Lucas was next door cleaning the drains. She looked as if she was in a bad mood. I think Mr and Mrs Lucas have got an unhappy marriage. Poor Mr Lucas!

   None of the teachers at school have noticed that I am an intellectual. They will be sorry when I am famous. There is a new girl in our class. She sits next to me in Geography. She is all right. Her name is Pandora, but she likes being called 'Box'. Don't ask me why. I might fall in love with her. It's time I fell in love, after all I am 13¾ years old.

Friday January 16th

Mr Lucas came round and offered to take my mother shopping in the car. They dropped me off at school. ... We saw Mrs Lucas on the way. She was carrying big bags of shopping. My mother waved, but Mrs Lucas couldn't wave back.

   It was Geography today so I sat next to Pandora for a whole hour. She looks better every day. I told her about her eyes being the same as the dog's. She asked what kind of dog it was. I told her it was a mongrel.

   I lent Pandora my blue felt-tip pen to colour round the British Isles.

   I think she appreciates these small attentions.

   I started *Origin of Species* today, but it's not as good as the television series. *Care of the Skin* is dead good. I have left it open on the pages about vitamins. I hope my mother takes the hint. I have left it on the kitchen table near the ashtray, so she is bound to see it.

   I have made an appointment about the spot. It has turned purple.

·····

Sunday January 25th

10 a.m. I am ill with all the worry, too weak to write much. Nobody has noticed I haven't eaten any breakfast.

2 p.m. Had two junior aspirins at midday and rallied a bit. Perhaps when I am famous and my diary is discovered people will understand the torment of being a 13¾-year-old undiscovered intellectual.

6 p.m. Pandora! My lost love!

Now I will never stroke your treacle hair! (Although my blue felt-tip is still at your disposal.)

8 p.m. Pandora! Pandora! Pandora!

10 p.m. Why? Why? Why?

Midnight. Had a crab-paste sandwich and a satsuma (for the good of my skin). Feel a bit better. I hope Nigel falls off his bike and is squashed flat by a lorry. I will never speak to him again. He knew I was in love with Pandora!

> **Notes** *Joined the library* (line 31): registered with a public library (a place where people can borrow books)
> *Origin of Species* (line 31): important scientific book by Charles Darwin
> *going on about* (line 32): talking constantly about
> *Pride and Prejudice* (line 32): 19th-century classic novel
> *was impressed* (line 33): (here) thought I was very clever
> *intellectual* (line 33): person of great intelligence
> *Mr and Mrs Lucas* (line 35 and 37): the Mole family's next-door neighbours
> *drains* (line 37): system of pipes and channels to carry dirty water away from houses
> *dropped me off* (line 46): let me get out of the car
> *mongrel* (line 50): dog of mixed or unknown breed
> *dead good* (line 54): (slang) very good
> *takes the hint* (line 55): understands what someone is trying to say
> *made an appointment* (line 57): (here) booked a time to see a doctor
> *junior aspirins* (line 61): painkiller pills for children
> *rallied a bit* (line 61): felt a little better
> *torment* (line 62): terrible pain
> *treacle* (line 65): (here) a golden-brown colour
> *at your disposal* (line 65): available for you to use
> *satsuma* (line 69): a type of small orange
> *Nigel* (line 70): Adrian's best friend

Working with the text

F True or false? Tick (✔) any true sentences and rewrite the false ones.

1. Adrian's teachers are impressed by his intelligence.
2. Adrian falls in love with Pandora at first sight.
3. Adrian's family don't pay much attention to him.
4. Adrian has three aspirins at midday.

G Reading between the lines

1. Why does Adrian borrow a book called *Care of the Skin*?
2. Why does he borrow *Pride and Prejudice*?
3. Why do you think Adrian's mother and Mr Lucas stop laughing when Adrian comes into the kitchen?
4. Why do you think Mrs Lucas 'looked as if she was in a bad mood' (line 37)?
5. Can you explain why Pandora likes being called 'Box'?
6. Why doesn't Mrs Lucas wave back at Mrs Mole?
7. Do you think Pandora likes being told that her eyes are like a mongrel dog's?
8. What is 'the hint' (line 55) that Adrian wants his mother to take?
9. What terrible thing happens between Friday and Sunday, and makes Adrian ill (line 59)?
10. How does Adrian feel about Nigel at midnight on Sunday 25th?

H Discussion

1. Adrian thinks he is an intellectual. Is an intellectual someone who …

   a can read difficult books?
   b can do complex maths?
   c can solve problems?

   What is your opinion?

2. 'It's time I fell in love' (line 42). Do you think there is a right time for …

   a falling in love?
   b leaving home?
   c getting married?
   d having children?
   e travelling round the world?

   Or should everybody choose their own time to do these things?

3. Do you like Adrian or not? What is good or bad about him? Does he make you laugh?

I Prediction

What do you think happens next? Tick (✔) as many as you like.

a Pandora loses interest in Nigel.
b Adrian falls in love with someone else.
c Adrian's spot gets better.
d Adrian's mother wears the green lurex apron.

The Secret Diary of Adrian Mole aged 13¾

Language work

A 'Eight days have gone by since Christmas Day' (line 11). *Since* and *for* are often used with the present perfect. Complete the sentences with either *since* or *for*.

1. It's been years _____ I last saw my cousins.
2. The doctor's been in the house _____ at least an hour.
3. I haven't been out to lunch _____ my birthday.
4. We've been waiting here _____ half an hour, you know.
5. The Fergusons? Oh, I've known them _____ about ten years.
6. _____ we bought the digital TV, we've hardly seen any programmes worth watching.

B 'I will be glad to get back to school' (line 21). This is an example of *will* used to make a prediction for the future. Complete the sentences to make predictions or promises, using *will*.

1. I think/the weather/probably be fine tomorrow.
2. I know/you/be very happy together.
3. I promise/I/help you as much as I can.
4. I'm sure/there/be no problems on the journey.
5. I don't think/I/be able to attend the wedding.
6. I have a feeling/nobody/come to my party!

C 'She sits next to me in Geography' (line 40). *Sits* is an example of the present simple, used to state a fact. Complete the sentences with the correct form of the present simple from the words in brackets.

1. The bedroom windows _____ east, so you _____ the sun rising in the morning. (face, see)
2. A bridge _____ the river, which _____ right down the valley. (cross, run)
3. Tourists _____ the caves because they _____ the thrill of being underground. (visit, enjoy)
4. The town _____ at the head of the lake, and the mountain _____ up behind it. (lie, rise)
5. People in Mediterranean countries _____ their olives and _____ them or _____ them to the local olive-oil factory. (pick, eat, sell)

Writing

Write your own diary (about 100 words) for an important day in your life. Say what happened and how you felt about it. Put the day's date at the top.

6 FRANK MCCOURT
1930–

Francis (Frank) McCourt was born in Brooklyn, New York City, USA, to Irish parents. When he was four, his family returned to Limerick, Ireland, where he grew up. At the age of nineteen he went back to the USA, where he had a series of low-paid jobs and spent every spare minute reading books from the public library. By studying hard, he managed to get a place at New York University and became a teacher. He taught English and other subjects for thirty years in various New York City high schools and city colleges, and after retiring from teaching, he sat down and began writing about his past. *Angela's Ashes* (1996) is the story of his childhood in Ireland; it became an international best-seller at once and went on to win the 1997 Pulitzer Prize, the Royal Society for Literature Award and two American awards. It was filmed by the British director Alan Parker in 1999, starring Robert Carlyle and Emily Watson. McCourt published his second book, *'Tis*, in 1999; this continues his autobiography, describing his life in the USA from 1949 onwards.

Frank McCourt lives with his wife in New York City and Connecticut, USA.

Other works by Frank McCourt: *'Tis*.

Angela's Ashes

This is the true story of Frank McCourt's childhood. From the age of four to nineteen he lived with his family in Limerick, Ireland. They were extremely poor, as there were several children and Frank's father could not always find regular work.

Before you read

What do you think life as a child in a poor Irish family was like in the 1930s and 1940s? What would the biggest problem have been? Tick (✔) as many as you like, and add your own ideas.

a not having enough food
b not having many toys to play with
c having no new clothes
d having no heating
e living in a very small house or flat
f not knowing when there will be any more money

Now read to the end of the text.

Think about these questions as you read. Is the text …

… exciting?   … funny?   … difficult?   … scary?   … sad?   … interesting?

When Dad gets a job Mam is cheerful and she sings,
> *Anyone can see why I wanted your kiss,*
> *It had to be and the reason is this*
> *Could it be true, someone like you*
> *Could love me, love me?*

When Dad brings home the first week's wages Mam is delighted she can pay the lovely Italian man in the grocery shop and she can hold her head up again because there's nothing worse in the world than to owe and be beholden to anyone. She cleans the kitchen, washes the mugs and plates, brushes crumbs and bits of food from the table, cleans out the icebox and orders a fresh block of ice from another Italian. ... She boils water on the stove and spends a day at a great tin tub washing our shirts and socks, diapers for the twins, our two sheets, our three towels. She hangs everything out on the clotheslines behind the apartment house and we can watch the clothes dance in wind and sun. She says you wouldn't want the neighbors to know what you have in the way of a wash but there's nothing like the sweetness of clothes dried by the sun.

When Dad brings home the first week's wages on a Friday night we know the weekend will be wonderful. On Saturday night Mam will boil water on the stove and wash us in the great tin tub and Dad will dry us. ... Mam will make hot cocoa and we'll be able to stay up while Dad tells us a story out of his head. ... On nights like that we can drift off to sleep knowing there will be a breakfast of eggs, fried tomatoes and fried bread, tea with lashings of sugar and milk and, later in the day, a big dinner of mashed potatoes, peas and ham, and a trifle Mam makes, layers of fruit and warm delicious custard on a cake soaked in sherry.

When Dad brings home the first week's wages and the weather is fine Mam takes us to the playground. She sits on a bench and talks to Minnie MacAdorey. She tells Minnie stories about characters in Limerick and Minnie tells her about characters in Belfast and they laugh because there are funny people in Ireland, North and South. Then they teach each other sad songs and Malachy and I leave the swings and seesaws to sit with them on the bench and sing. .....

When we go home Mam makes tea and bread and jam or mashed potatoes with butter and salt. Dad drinks the tea and eats nothing. Mam says, God above, How can you work all day and not eat? He says, The tea is enough. She says, You'll ruin your health, and he tells her again that food is a shock to the system. He drinks his tea and tells us stories and shows us letters and words in the *Daily News* or he smokes a cigarette, stares at the wall, runs his tongue over his lips.

When Dad's job goes into the third week he does not bring home the wages. On Friday night we wait for him and Mam gives us bread and tea. ... Other men with jobs are home already and having eggs for dinner because you can't have meat on a Friday. You can hear the families talking upstairs and downstairs and down the hall and Bing Crosby is singing on the radio, *Brother, can you spare a dime?*

Malachy and I play with the twins. We know Mam won't sing *Anyone can see why I wanted your kiss*. She sits at the kitchen table talking to herself, What am I going to do? till it's late.

FRANK MCCOURT

Notes
Mam (line 1): (Irish) Mum, Mother
cheerful (line 1): happy
wages (line 6): pay
grocery shop (line 7): shop selling all kinds of food
be beholden to (line 8): (old-fashioned) feel guilty because you owe something to someone
mugs (line 9): large cups
icebox (line 10): old-fashioned kind of fridge, a box holding a large piece of ice
another Italian (line 10): many shopkeepers in Limerick were Italian
diapers (line 12): (American) nappies, cloths for babies' bottoms
twins (line 12): two children born from the same pregnancy
neighbors (line 14): (American spelling) neighbours, people living nearby
lashings of (line 22): lots of
trifle (line 23): a dessert, a sweet dish made with fruit and cake
Minnie MacAdorey (line 26): a neighbour and friend who had lived in Belfast, Northern Ireland
Malachy (line 29): Frank's younger brother
swings and seesaws (line 29): things for children to play on in a playground
a shock to the system (line 34): difficult for the body to accept
stares (line 36): looks fixedly
meat on a Friday (line 39): many Roman Catholics don't eat meat on Fridays
Bing Crosby (line 41): American singer and film star (1904–1977)
dime (line 41): (American) small coin, also called ten cents

Working with the text

Do you like the text? Why or why not?

A Answer the questions.

1 When does Frank's mother become cheerful?
2 Does she have any machines to help her with the housework?
3 What happens on Saturday night?
4 When they have enough money, what do the family have **a** for breakfast? **b** for dinner?
5 How does Mrs McCourt feel about her husband not eating?
6 What happens in the third week?

B Reading between the lines

1 What kind of song does Frank's mother sing?
2 How does she usually pay for food in shops – in cash or in some other way?
3 Why do you think she does so much housework on one day?
4 What does 'you wouldn't want the neighbors to know what you have in the way of a wash' (line 14) tell us about Mrs McCourt?
5 How often do the children have a bath?
6 How does Mrs McCourt feel when her husband doesn't bring home his wages?

C The verbs on the left (1–10) are from the first two paragraphs of the text. Match them with their objects (a–j). Try to do it from memory, then check with the text.

1	gets	a	the lovely Italian man
2	brings home	b	crumbs from the table
3	pay	c	everything out on the clotheslines
4	hold		
5	cleans	d	the mugs and plates
6	washes	e	the first week's wages
7	brushes	f	water
8	orders	g	a fresh block of ice
9	boils	h	a job
10	hangs	i	the kitchen
		j	her head up

D Match the nouns, to make pairs of words from the text. They are all linked with *and*. Try to do it from memory first, then check with the text.

1	wind	a	seesaws
2	north	b	downstairs
3	swings	c	jam
4	bread	d	south
5	letters	e	sun
6	upstairs	f	words

E Discussion

1 What do you know now about the characters of Mr and Mrs McCourt? Are they happy together, do you think?

Angela's Ashes

2 What is life like for Frank and his brothers when their father doesn't bring home any wages? How different is it from the times when he *does* bring wages home?

3 What do you think has happened to Frank's father on the third Friday night? Do you think he should try harder to make sure his family have enough money to eat well? Or do you understand how difficult it can be, if you are the person responsible for feeding your family?

F Prediction

What do you think happens next? Tick (✔) as many as you like.

a Frank's father arrives home late, with no money.
b The police come and tell Mrs McCourt there has been an accident.
c A kind neighbour pays for the family's evening meal.
d Mrs McCourt goes out to look for her husband.
e Mrs McCourt takes the children and leaves her husband.

Language work

A 'She sits on a bench' (line 26). *On* is a preposition of place, and so are *at*, *in* and *to*. Complete these sentences with the correct preposition from the box.

| at   on   in   to |

1 I was _____ home all day yesterday.
2 The post office is _____ an old building in South Street.
3 My friends arrived _____ France last week.
4 The doctor hung his coat _____ the back of the door.
5 I'm flying _____ Lisbon tonight.
6 I live _____ 48 Dancing Lane.
7 Put the plates _____ the table, will you?
8 I can't stop – I'm just off _____ the dentist's.

B There are a lot of words connected with food in this text. Complete the sentences about food and ways of cooking with the correct word from the text.

1 You can add sugar to tea, and drink it with either lemon or _____.

2 _____ tomatoes are tomatoes cooked in oil in a frying-pan.

3 Potatoes probably taste better if you add a little _____ to the pan while boiling them.

4 _____ are the only food you can eat boiled, fried, poached or scrambled. You can also bake them!

5 There's nothing like the smell of freshly-baked _____, straight out of the oven. You can eat it hot, with _____ and jam.

Role play

Student A: You are telling your friend (Student B) about your childhood – how poor and hungry you always were. You're enjoying Student B's sympathy, so you exaggerate a little, and your story becomes sadder and sadder!

Student B: At first you believed Student A's sad story about his or her terrible childhood, but soon you realise that it is not true. Start telling Student A about *your* childhood, and make it sound even worse than Student A's. See who can tell the saddest story.

7 LEWIS CARROLL
1832–1898

Charles Lutwidge Dodgson was born in Daresbury, Cheshire, England. He studied at Oxford University and became a lecturer in mathematics. Although he never married and did not have any children of his own, he enjoyed the company of other people's children. He invented the stories which eventually became *Alice's Adventures in Wonderland* (1865) to tell to a little girl called Alice, the daughter of one of his Oxford colleagues. He wrote under the pen name of Lewis Carroll. *Through the Looking-Glass* was written later, after a meeting with a distant cousin – another small girl, whose name was also Alice. These two books have become classics of English literature, read with great enjoyment by both adults and children.

Lewis Carroll lived in the north of England for much of his life.

Other works by Lewis Carroll: *Through the Looking-Glass, The Hunting of the Snark, Rhyme and Reason, Sylvie and Bruno.*

Alice's Adventures in Wonderland

Alice is a young girl who has discovered an exciting new world underground. She was sitting on the riverbank, when suddenly a White Rabbit hurried past her, and she followed him down his rabbit-hole. Since then she has met all sorts of strange, talking animals – a Mouse, a Duck, a Dodo, a Crab, a Caterpillar, a Pigeon, a Fish and a Cheshire Cat – and had some unusual experiences. Once she drank from a bottle, which made her become much smaller, and then ate a cake, which made her grow much larger. It is hard to know what will happen next in Wonderland! Now she is coming closer to the March Hare's house. Here she will meet the March Hare, the Hatter and the Dormouse.

Before you read

What do you think will happen to Alice at the March Hare's house? Tick (✔) as many as you like.

a The March Hare will play a trick on her.
b She will join the March Hare and his friends at teatime.
c The Hatter will explain more about life in Wonderland.
d The March Hare and the Hatter will be very polite to her, as she is a guest.

Now read to the end of the text.

Think about these questions as you read. Is the text …

… exciting?   … funny?   … difficult?   … scary?   … sad?   … interesting?

There was a table set out under a tree in front of the house, and the March Hare and the Hatter were having tea at it: a Dormouse was sitting between them, fast asleep, and the other two were using it as a cushion, resting their elbows on it, and talking over its head. 'Very uncomfortable for the Dormouse,' thought Alice; 'only, as it's asleep, I suppose it doesn't mind.'

The table was a large one, but the three were all crowded together at one corner of it. 'No room! No room!' they cried out when they saw Alice coming. 'There's *plenty* of room!' said Alice indignantly, and she sat down in a large arm-chair at one end of the table.

'Have some wine,' the March Hare said in an encouraging tone.

Alice looked all round the table, but there was nothing on it but tea. 'I don't see any wine,' she remarked.

'There isn't any,' said the March Hare.

'Then it wasn't very civil of you to offer it,' said Alice angrily.

'It wasn't very civil of you to sit down without being invited,' said the March Hare.

'I didn't know it was *your* table,' said Alice: 'it's laid for a great many more than three.'

'Your hair wants cutting,' said the Hatter. He had been looking at Alice for some time with great curiosity, and this was his first speech.

'You should learn not to make personal remarks,' Alice said with some severity: 'it's very rude.'

The Hatter opened his eyes very wide on hearing this; but all he *said* was 'Why is a raven like a writing-desk?'

'Come, we shall have some fun now!' thought Alice. 'I'm glad they've begun asking riddles – I believe I can guess that,' she added aloud.

'Do you mean that you think you can find out the answer to it?' said the March Hare.

'Exactly so,' said Alice.

'Then you should say what you mean,' the March Hare went on.

'I do,' Alice hastily replied; 'at least – at least I mean what I say – that's the same thing, you know.'

'Not the same thing a bit!' said the Hatter. 'Why, you might just as well say that "I see what I eat" is the same thing as "I eat what I see"!'

'You might just as well say,' added the March Hare, 'that "I like what I get" is the same thing as "I get what I like"!'

'You might just as well say,' added the Dormouse, which seemed to be talking in its sleep, 'that "I breathe when I sleep" is the same thing as "I sleep when I breathe"!'

'It *is* the same thing with you,' said the Hatter, and here the conversation dropped.

LEWIS CARROLL

Notes *Hare* (line 1): animal like a large rabbit, which is especially wild and excitable in March
Hatter (line 2): person who makes hats
(Note: There are two expressions in English: 'as mad as a March hare' and 'as mad as a hatter')
Dormouse (line 2): type of small mouse which spends a lot of time sleeping
room (line 7): (here) space
indignantly (line 8): crossly
civil (line 14): polite
wants cutting (line 18): needs cutting, needs to be cut
great curiosity (line 19): strong desire to know about something
with some severity (line 20): sharply, crossly, strictly
raven (line 23): very large black bird
riddles (line 25): questions or puzzles; you need to think about them to find the answers
hastily (line 30): quickly
you might just as well say (line 32): it would be equally correct to say
the conversation dropped (line 38): they stopped talking

Working with the text

Do you like the text? Why or why not?

A Answer the questions.

1 How many people and animals are sitting at the table before Alice arrives?
2 What is on the table?
3 Why is Alice angry with the March Hare?
4 Why does Alice speak sharply to the Hatter?
5 Why is Alice pleased when the Hatter asks a riddle?

B Look at the pairs of sentences on the left (1–5). In each pair **a** has a different meaning from **b**. Match each sentence with its correct meaning (i or ii).

1 **a** I can guess the answer.
  b I can find out the answer.
  i I'll think of a possible answer myself.
  ii I can look up information to get the answer.

2 **a** I say what I mean.
  b I mean what I say.
  i My feelings match my words.
  ii I'm careful to use exactly the right words.

3 **a** I see what I eat.
  b I eat what I see.
  i I look at whatever is on my plate.
  ii I eat all the food in front of me.

4 **a** I like what I get.
  b I get what I like.
  i I always get anything I want.
  ii I enjoy all the things I manage to get.

5 **a** I breathe when I sleep.
  b I sleep when I breathe.
  i All the time I'm asleep, I'm breathing.
  ii All the time I'm breathing, I'm asleep.

C True or false? Tick (✔) any true sentences and rewrite the false ones.

1 The March Hare and his friends think there is plenty of room for Alice.
2 The table is laid for three people to have tea.
3 The Hatter likes Alice's long hair.
4 The Dormouse spends most of the time sleeping.

D Reading between the lines

1 Why do you think the March Hare offers wine to Alice, when there isn't any? Is he just mad? Or is he trying to tell her something about politeness? If so, what?
2 Why do you think the Hatter 'opened his eyes very wide' (line 22)?
3 What does the Hatter mean when he says to the Dormouse, 'It *is* the same thing with you' (line 38)? Why does the conversation stop after that?

E Discussion

1 We discover later that the Hatter and the March Hare don't know the answer to the riddle, so why do you think the Hatter asks it? For fun? To annoy Alice? Or for some other reason?
2 Is it important to be careful with language, like the March Hare and the Hatter? For example, if you say, 'I work to live', how different is that from 'I live to work'? Does a change in word order make a difference in *your* language?
3 This text is taken from a chapter called 'A Mad Tea-Party'. What is mad about it?

35

Alice's Adventures in Wonderland

F Prediction

What do you think happens next? Underline one of the alternatives in italics.

1 The Hatter *continues the conversation/gets up and leaves.*
2 Alice *thinks of an answer to the riddle/tries to understand a story told by the Dormouse.*
3 The March Hare *offers Alice some tea/passes Alice some cake.*

Language work

A 'There's plenty of room!' (line 7). *Room* is used as an uncountable noun here, meaning *space*. Decide whether these words are uncountable or countable. Write U for uncountable and C for countable.

bread	water	information
meat	car	advice
furniture	news	people
book	chair	vegetable
letter	fruit	sugar

Now complete the sentences by choosing the correct form of the verb in brackets. Remember to use a singular verb after uncountable nouns.

1 Your advice (is/are) always useful.
2 The news (was/were) awful yesterday.
3 The information (is/are) just what I wanted.
4 These people (come/comes) from the next village.
5 Your furniture (look/looks) expensive!
6 Do you think this meat (smell/smells) bad?

B '... said Alice angrily' (line 14). *Angrily* is an adverb. Most adverbs are made by adding *-ly* to an adjective: *angry + -ly = angrily* (note the spelling change). Complete the sentences with the correct adverb, using the word in brackets.

1 This train's going very _____! (slow)
2 They got married and lived _____ ever after. (happy)
3 'I'm very sorry,' Aileen said _____. (sad)
4 You can _____ find the way if you use a map. (easy)
5 _____ Helen saw her cousin running towards her. (sudden)
6 The dog looked _____ at its empty bowl. (hungry)

Now play the Adverb Game. Think of an adverb, and act it out in front of your friends. For example, you are thinking of *proudly*. Walk around with your head held high and a confident, self-important smile on your lips. The first person to guess your adverb takes the next turn.

C Here are some riddles. Can you work out the answers?

1 What has a neck but cannot swallow?
2 When is a car not a car?
3 What's the difference between a train driver and a teacher?
4 Why did the thief take a bath?
5 Why didn't the ghost go to the party?
6 What's the difference between ignorance and indifference?

Do you know any riddles? Can you translate one from your own language?

Writing

You are writing a short story (about 100 words) for a competition. It must have the title **A Mad Tea Party**. You can include any of the following:

a pink elephant
a talking horse
yellow coffee
a legless chair

a cat wearing trousers
a dancing tree
a house made of bread
a hat made of gold

three flying pigs
a laughing lion
tomato cake
a teapot with no handle

8 DAVID HEMPLEMAN-ADAMS WITH ROBERT UHLIG
1956–

David Hempleman-Adams was born in Swindon, Wiltshire, England. He won a gold medal in the Duke of Edinburgh Award Scheme, which gave him an early interest in adventuring. Since 1984, he has become the first man to walk solo and unsupported to the magnetic North Pole, and the first Briton to walk alone and unaided to the South Pole. He has also climbed the 'Seven Summits' – the seven highest mountains in all seven continents. His book *Toughing It Out* is the best-selling account of his walk to the South Pole. In early March 1998 he started a journey to the geographic North Pole which he hoped would make him the first person to score the explorers' Grand Slam – this involves walking to the geographic North and South Poles and climbing the Seven Summits. *Walking on Thin Ice* was published in 1998. In 2003 he was the first person to cross the Atlantic Ocean in an open-basket hot-air balloon. He is a businessman and lives near Bath, in the south-west of England, with his wife and three daughters.

Robert Uhlig was born in Hertfordshire, England. He is a journalist, working for *The Daily Telegraph* in London, and has won awards for his magazine articles and editing. In March 1998 he went with David Hempleman-Adams and Rune Gjeldnes to base camp at Resolute Bay in the High Arctic, to write about their attempt to walk to the North Pole. He lives in London.

Other works by David Hempleman-Adams: *Toughing It Out*.

Walking on Thin Ice

This is a factual account of David Hempleman-Adams' 1998 journey on foot across the floating ice to the North Pole. He is walking with a Norwegian partner, Rune Gjeldnes. Both men are pulling sledges carrying all their food and equipment. This text is headed:

Day 26: Monday 30 March
Temperature: –38°C
Windchill: –58°C
Nautical miles covered so far: 121.75
Nautical miles to go (in a straight line): 293.25

Before you read

Which of these things would you be most afraid of, on a journey like this? Tick (✔) as many as you like, and add some of your own ideas.

- frostbite
- heart attack
- polar bears
- freezing to death
- dying of hunger
- breaking a bone
- getting lost
- falling through the ice

Now read the text up to 'I won't recover from this.' (line 24).

Think about these questions as you read. Is the text ...

... exciting?   ... funny?   ... difficult?   ... scary?   ... sad?   ... interesting?

We set off after breakfast and within an hour we encounter disaster. The nightmare that has been haunting me for fourteen years and which stopped recurring only eighteen months ago comes back to torment me, and this time it is real. It is probably the worst single moment I've had in fifteen years of polar exploration.

At the first lead we come to Rune goes ahead with his sledge behind him, and I follow in his tracks. One moment I am crossing what appears to be a solid section of ice, the next I have fallen through the ice into the water with my skis on. In the white-out I had not noticed that a hanging cornice of snow at the edge of a section of fresh ice was only an inch or so thick. Now I am up to my waist in the Arctic Ocean and panicking. As I fall, I rip my ice-spikes from around my neck, attempt to dig the two titanium nails into the nearest piece of white ice I can spot, and shout to Rune, who is about nine feet away and seemingly oblivious. I try to swim, something I find difficult at the best of times, but I cannot move my legs with my skis still attached to my feet. I am sinking, aware that I'll lose strength in the cold water and slip under the ice if I don't do something soon.

Rune has already heard me go, but in the slow-motion world I am enveloped in he has not reacted yet. I have heard that people's lives often flash in front of them shortly before they die, and at this moment it seems as if a brief summary of the last few months is being projected inside my eyes. I see the preparations in Resolute, our departure from Ward Hunt Island and the weeks we have spent together in the tent. Most worryingly, I see the frostbite on my nose, toes and fingers spreading, and this plunge into the Arctic Ocean ending my bid for the North Pole and the Grand Slam. This is it, I think for the second time in three days. The expedition is over. I won't recover from this.

But before I know it the world around me speeds up and Rune is in front of me, hauling me out of the −4°C clutches of the Arctic Ocean. He drags me on to an ice floe, where I lie, gasping for breath, my trouser legs already freezing solid like stovepipes. I want Rune to put up the tent double-quick so that I can get out of my sodden clothing and crawl inside my sleeping-bag, but he advises against it. 'The best thing you can do is to keep walking,' Rune says. 'Then your body warmth will dry out your clothes from the inside.' It sounds unlikely to me. I am terrified that my frostbite will now spread across my entire foot and up my legs. I need to get my clothes off, I insist. 'Trust me, David, it has happened to me many times before. If you stop now, the water will freeze into your clothes and you will never get the ice out of them. You must keep walking.'

So we head off northwards again, me with my knees shaking for at least the next two hours.

DAVID HEMPLEMAN-ADAMS

> **Notes** [Some of the words and expressions are dealt with in *Working with the text*.]
>
> *lead* (line 5): (rhymes with *seed*) channel of water between the ice
> *sledge* (line 5): container or carrier for people or goods, pulled over snow or ice
> *white-out* (line 7): when it's difficult to see, because there is heavy cloud cover and snow-covered ground
> *cornice* (line 8): (here) overhanging ledge of snow
> *an inch* (line 9): about 2.5 centimetres
> *ice-spikes* (line 10): pointed metal nails for holding on to ice
> *titanium* (line 11): strong white metal
> *nine feet* (line 12): just under three metres
> *oblivious* (line 12): not noticing
> *frostbite* (line 21): when parts of the body are damaged by severe cold
> *hauling* (line 26): pulling
> *ice floe* (line 26): large piece of floating ice
> *stovepipes* (line 28): metal pipes to take smoke away from a stove or heater
> *sodden* (line 29): soaking wet

Working with the text

A The words on the left (1–12) are from the text. Find them, then match them to their approximate meanings (a–l).

1 encounter
2 disaster
3 nightmare
4 recurring
5 torment
6 ahead
7 rip
8 attempt
9 spot
10 sinking
11 enveloped
12 brief

a cause mental suffering
b meet
c short
d going down
e see
f a bad dream
g wrapped
h a bad accident
i happening again and again
j try
k pull
l in front

B Answer the questions.

1 How long has David been exploring the Poles?
2 What happens when David crosses a section of ice, following Rune? Why does this happen?
3 Which three things does David do, in this dangerous situation?
4 Is David a good swimmer? How do you know?
5 Why do the last few weeks of the trip flash before David's eyes?
6 What is David most worried about?

C Reading between the lines

1 What do you think the nightmare is, which has haunted David for fourteen years?
2 Why do you think David is in a panic when he falls into the water?

3 Why do you think Rune does not notice at first that David has fallen in?
4 How close do you think David is to death, before Rune comes to help him?

D Discussion

1 How would you feel about going on a trip like this? How would you prepare for it?
2 Why do you think David chose a Norwegian as his partner on the trip? Who would *you* choose if you went on a trip like this?

Now read to the end of the text.

Do you like the text? Why or why not?

E Find expressions from paragraph 4 which mean the same as:

1 pulling me out
2 extra fast
3 wet clothes
4 my advice to you is
5 doesn't seem probable
6 very frightened

F True or false? Tick (✔) any true sentences and rewrite the false ones.

1 Rune jumps into the water to save David.
2 David's arms are frozen solid.
3 David wants to get inside the tent.
4 Rune advises David to keep moving.
5 David accepts his friend's advice at once.
6 Rune has fallen into freezing water before.

39

Walking on Thin Ice

G Reading between the lines

1 Why do you think 'the world around (David) speeds up' (line 25)? Does this really happen, or is it just an impression?
2 Why does David want to 'crawl inside (his) sleeping-bag' (line 29)?

H Discussion

What makes people walk to the North or South Pole or climb Mount Everest? Do you admire them, or do you think they are slightly mad?

I Prediction

What do you think happens next? Tick (✔) as many as you like.

a David dies of the cold.
b Rune and David reach the North Pole.
c Rune and David give up this time and try again the following year.
d Rune falls into the water and David saves him.

Language work

A 'If you stop now, the water will freeze into your clothes' (line 33). This is an example of a first conditional. Match the two parts of first conditional sentences, and put the verbs in the correct form. Remember that *unless* means *if not*.

1 If you (help) me with the painting,
2 If my train (be) late,
3 We (eat) outside
4 I think I (have) some soup,
5 I (not go) to the party

a if the weather (be) nice.
b unless I (be) invited.
c we (get) the job done faster.
d I (phone) you to let you know.
e unless there (be) meat in it.

Now think of three first conditional sentences of your own.

B 'We set off after breakfast' (line 1). *Set off* is a phrasal verb meaning *start a journey*. Put these phrasal verbs, in the correct form, into the sentences below.

| look after   take off   look up |
| call for   grow up |

1 Is your plane _____ from Luton or Heathrow?
2 I'll _____ you tonight, if you like, on my way into town.
3 You're working far too hard. You should _____ yourself a bit better.
4 I'll probably _____ what I want to know on the internet.
5 She _____ a lot since you last saw her.

Which is your favourite phrasal verb, out of all the ones you know? Put it into a sentence of your own.

Role play

Student A: You are planning an exciting and adventurous trip, driving across the Sahara Desert. You need a group of eight people, in two jeeps, and you are trying to decide exactly who to take with you. You are talking to your friend, Student B, about the trip. You think your friend may not be the right kind of person to join the group. Find out how useful your friend would be (what about cooking, first aid, driving, repairing a jeep, map-reading, speaking Arabic? Is he or she fit and healthy, and OK in the heat?), and explain the risks.

Student B: The idea of the trip fascinates you and you would love to go. Be very enthusiastic. Try not to let your friend know that you have a weak heart and can't drive. You are very good at mending bikes, you can cook steaks really well and you speak excellent Portuguese. Try to persuade Student A that what the group really needs is someone like you, who can tell jokes all day long to keep everyone cheerful.

Writing

This is part of a letter you receive from your English friend Linda.

I have just started rock-climbing – it's great! What do you do in your free time?

Write a letter (about 100 words) to Linda, answering her question.

9 ROBERT HARRIS
1957–

Robert Dennis Harris was born in Nottingham, England. He studied English at Cambridge University and worked as a journalist for fourteen years. First he was a reporter on the BBC's *Newsnight* and *Panorama* programmes, then he became political editor of *The Observer*, a quality Sunday newspaper. Finally he wrote columns for *The Sunday Times* and for *The Daily Telegraph*. In 1992 his first novel, *Fatherland,* was published. It was translated into twenty-five languages and became a best-seller throughout the world; it was also made into a film in 1994. In 1995 he wrote *Enigma*, which also became a best-seller and was filmed in 2001.

Robert Harris lives in Berkshire, England, with his wife and their four children.

Other works by Robert Harris: (fiction) *Fatherland, Archangel, Pompeii*; (non-fiction) *A Higher Form of Killing* (with Jeremy Paxman), *Gotcha!, The Making of Neil Kinnock, Selling Hitler, Good and Faithful Servant*.

Enigma

It is March 1943, during the Second World War. Nazi Germany's U-boats are regularly attacking and sinking the American and British convoys of ships carrying much-needed food across the Atlantic to the Allies in Europe. If only the Allies could break the Germans' codes and read their signals, the convoys could be protected. Britain has set up a top-secret intelligence centre at Bletchley Park in Buckinghamshire, where the best brains in the country are trying to crack the codes.

This part of the story is told from the point of view of Tom Jericho, a brilliant young mathematician who is working at Bletchley Park. He has a lot to worry about – the woman he loves, Claire Romilly, who also works at Bletchley Park, has disappeared, and he is afraid that one of the people working with him may be a spy, sending information to the Germans.

Before you read

What do you think the title *Enigma* means? Tick (✔) as many as you like.

a   a puzzle or a mystery
b   the name of a ship
c   a kind of mathematics
d   the name of a code machine
e   a mysterious woman

Now read the text up to 'Hang her?' (line 26).

Think about these questions as you read. Is the text …

… exciting?   … funny?   … difficult?   … scary?   … sad?   … interesting?

Eleven hours had passed since his conversation with Wigram. They might have found her by now. More likely, she would have turned up, either at the cottage or the hut – wide-eyed and wondering, darlings, what on earth the fuss was all about.

He was on the point of turning away from the window when his eye was caught by a movement at the far end of the engine shed. Was it a large animal of some sort, or a big man crawling on all fours? He squinted through the sooty glass but the thing was too far away for him to make it out exactly, so he fetched his telescope from the bottom of the wardrobe. The window sash was stuck but a few heavy blows from the heel of his hand were enough to raise it six inches. He knelt and rested the telescope on the sill. At first he couldn't find anything to focus on amid the dizzying crisscross of tracks but then, suddenly, it was filling his eye – an Alsatian dog as big as a calf, sniffing under the wheels of a goods wagon. He shifted the telescope a fraction to his left and there was a policeman dressed in a greatcoat that came down below his knees. Two policemen, in fact, and a second dog, on a leash.

He watched the little group for several minutes as they searched the empty train. Then the two teams split up, one passing further up the tracks and the other moving out of sight towards the little railway cottages opposite. He snapped the telescope shut.

Four men and two dogs for the railway yard. Say, a couple more teams to cover the station platforms. How many in the town? Twenty? And in the surrounding countryside?

'Got a photo of her? Something recent?'

He tapped the telescope against his cheek.

They must be watching every port and railway station in the country.

What would they do if they caught her?

Hang her?

Come on, Jericho. He could practically hear his housemaster's voice at his elbow. *Brace up, boy.*

Get through it somehow.

Wash. Shave. Dress. Make a little bundle of dirty laundry and leave it on the bed for Mrs Armstrong, more in hope than expectation. Go downstairs. Endure attempts to make polite conversation. ... Be introduced to two of the other guests: Miss Quince ... and Noakes .... Avoid all further conversation. Chew toast as stale as cardboard. Drink tea as grey and watery as a February sky. Half-listen to the wireless news: 'Moscow Radio reports the Russian Third Army under General Vatutin is making a strong defence of Kharkov in the face of the renewed German offensive ...'

At ten to eight Mrs Armstrong came in with the morning post. ... Two letters for Miss Jobey, a postcard for Miss Quince, a bill from Heffers bookshop for Mr Noakes and nothing at all for Mr Jericho – oh, except this, which she'd found when she came down and which must have been put through the door some time in the night.

He held it carefully. The envelope was poor quality, official-issue stuff, his name printed on it in blue ink, with 'By hand, Strictly Personal' added underneath and double-underlined.

Notes [Some of the words and expressions are dealt with in *Working with the text*.]

Wigram (line 1): Mr Wigram is an important person in the British Foreign Office
cottage (line 2): small house in the countryside
hut (line 3): small wooden buildings – the codebreakers worked in huts
fuss (line 3): bother, worry, trouble
engine shed (line 5): large building where train engines are kept
crawling on all fours (line 6): walking on hands and knees, like an animal
squinted (line 6): looked through slightly closed eyes, to see better
sooty (line 6): dirty from smoke
window sash (line 8): rope for lifting an old-fashioned window, to open it
blows from ... his hand (line 8): he hit it several times with his hand
six inches (line 9): about fifteen centimetres
sill (line 10): shelf at the bottom of a window
amid (line 10): among, in the middle of
crisscross of tracks (line 10): tracks or lines crossing each other in different directions
Alsatian dog (line 11): large wolf-like dog
leash (line 14): line or rope tied to a dog to control it
hang (line 26): put someone to death by hanging them from a rope round their neck
housemaster (line 27): teacher at a boarding school
Brace up (line 28): (old-fashioned) cheer up, be brave
dirty laundry (line 30): clothes that need washing
Mrs Armstrong (line 31): Tom's landlady, who owns the house where he is staying
endure (line 31): put up with, tolerate but not enjoy
cardboard (line 34): thin stiff board made from paper

Working with the text

Do you like the text so far? Why or why not?

A Choose the best way of completing the sentences, **a**, **b** or **c**.

1 The view from Tom's window is of a
  a police station.   b coach station.
  c railway station.
2 Tom uses a telescope to
  a study the stars.   b watch a search party.
  c look at wild animals.
3 a The police   b The Germans
  c Spies are watching every port and station in the country.
4 If they catch 'her', Tom thinks she will probably
  a be put to death.   b go to prison.
  c lose her job.

B The words and expressions on the left (1–9) are from the text, some with small changes. Find them in the text, then match them to their approximate meanings (a–i).

1 turn up	a see
2 on the point of	b look at carefully
3 make out	c arrive unexpectedly
4 stuck	d separate
5 focus on	e move a little
6 dizzying	f young cow
7 calf	g confusing
8 shift a fraction	h unable to move
9 split up	i about to

C Reading between the lines

1 Who do you think the police are looking for?
2 What do you think Tom's conversation with Wigram was about?
3 Who is 'wide-eyed and wondering' (line 3)?
4 Why does Tom think there will be even more search parties all over the country?
5 Who do you think says, 'Got a photo of her?' (line 22). Why do they need a recent photo?
6 Why do you think 'they' might hang her? What do you think she has done?

Now read to the end of the text.

D Answer the questions.

1 Is Tom sure that Mrs Armstrong will do his washing? How do you know?
2 Who are the 'guests' (line 32)? Are they at a party, or do they all live there?
3 What is life like in Mrs Armstrong's house? What is wrong with the toast and the tea?
4 In your own words, say what is happening according to the radio news.
5 Who receives a postcard?
6 Who receives a bill for some books?
7 What does Tom receive? Did it come by post? If not, how did it come?

Enigma

E Reading between the lines

1 How does Tom feel when he says, 'Get through it somehow' (line 29) and why?
2 Why do you think he wants to 'avoid all further conversation' (line 33)? Give at least two possible reasons.

F Discussion

1 Do you think that loving another person is more important than loving your country? If Tom had to choose between Claire and Britain, which do you think he would choose? Which *should* he choose, in your opinion?
2 Spies sometimes lie or pretend to be people they are not. Is this acceptable? Should spies be punished if they are caught? If so, how?

G Prediction

1 Who do you think Tom's letter is from? Choose **a**, **b**, **c** or **d**.

   a Claire Romilly   **c** Wigram
   b Claire's father   **d** a friend of Claire's

2 Does the letter give information about ...

   a a meeting?   **c** a missing person?
   b a code?   **d** a mistake that was made?

3 What do you think happens next? Tom ...

   a finds Claire.   **c** is trapped by a spy.
   b breaks the code.   **d** is wrongly arrested by the police.

Language work

A 'What would they do if they caught her?' (line 25). This is an example of a second conditional. Match these parts of second conditional sentences.

1 Would she ever forgive Bill
2 If there were any more biscuits,
3 Would anyone mind
4 If you won one million dollars,
5 If I had my bike with me,
6 What kind of flat would you live in

a I'd probably eat them!
b what would you spend it on?
c I'd cycle there.
d if he told her the truth?
e if you had the choice?
f if we opened the window?

Make two second conditional sentences about yourself.

B 'He could practically hear his housemaster's voice' (line 27). *Practically* here means *almost*, *nearly*, and it's an important word, because it means Tom *couldn't* hear his housemaster's voice – he could only hear it in his imagination. Put *practically* in the correct place in the following sentences, to show that the action *didn't* or *couldn't* happen, although it was close to happening.

1 I crashed the car.
2 She fell over.
3 He broke his leg.
4 I could see the finishing line.
5 Her little son could read when he was two!

Now make two sentences of your own, using *practically* in this way.

Role Play

Student A: You have been worried about your boyfriend, Student B. He disappeared a few days ago without telling you and has only just returned. Tell him how angry you are with him. Ask him why he didn't tell you where he was going, or keep in touch, where he was all that time and who he was with!

Student B: You went away for a while because you needed some time and space on your own. You hate being questioned so closely about your movements, and you are beginning to think your girlfriend is far too possessive and jealous. You don't feel you need to give her any answers. It's difficult for you to stay calm when she keeps asking you question after question!

Writing

In the story, Tom Jericho received a letter. Decide who you think wrote it, then write the letter. In your letter (about 100 words) say:

- why you are writing
- what information you want to give Tom
- what you want to happen next.

10 ANNE TYLER
1941–

Anne Tyler was born in Minneapolis, Minnesota, USA, and grew up in Raleigh, North Carolina. Having worked as a librarian at an American and a Canadian university, she finally settled in Baltimore, Maryland, USA, and started writing full-time. Her first novel, *If Morning Ever Comes*, came out in 1964, and she continued to publish novels, but it was not until about ten years later that her fellow Americans began to appreciate her writing. Her book *Dinner at the Homesick Restaurant* (1982) was a national best-seller, and her highly successful novel *The Accidental Tourist* (1985) was made into a film in 1988, starring William Hurt and Kathleen Turner. She won a Pulitzer Prize in 1989 for *Breathing Lessons*. She has also written many short stories.

Anne Tyler lives with her family in Baltimore, USA, where her novels are set.

Other works by Anne Tyler: *If Morning Ever Comes, The Tin Can Tree, The Clock Winder, Celestial Navigation, Searching for Caleb, Dinner at the Homesick Restaurant, Breathing Lessons, Saint Maybe, Ladder of Years, A Patchwork Planet, Back When We Were Grownups, The Amateur Marriage.*

The Accidental Tourist

Macon Leary is a careful, cautious man, who enjoys having a routine, or what he calls 'a system' – finding the best possible way of doing things and then always doing things that way. He earns his money from writing guidebooks for North American travellers (the *Accidental Tourist* series), recommending all the places in a foreign city where homesick Americans can find their favourite food and drink, so that they can forget they're abroad, and imagine they're safely back home again. His publisher is a man called Julian Edge.

Recently Macon's young son Ethan has died and, partly as a result of this, Macon's wife Sarah has left him. He is surprised to find that he's having some difficulty getting used to living alone. He has just returned home to Baltimore after a business trip to England, where he was finding out information for a new edition of *Accidental Tourist in England*.

Before you read

What do you think Macon finds most difficult, now that Sarah has left? Tick (✔) as many as you like.

a walking his dog
b keeping cheerful
c finding time to write
d doing the housework
e finding someone to talk to
f remembering to wash and shave

Now read to the end of the text.

Think about these questions as you read. Is the text …

… exciting?   … funny?   … difficult?   … scary?   … sad?   … interesting?

When the phone rang, Macon dreamed it was Ethan. He dreamed Ethan was calling from camp, wondering why they'd never come to get him. 'But we thought you were dead,' Macon said, and Ethan said – in that clear voice of his that cracked on the high notes – 'Why would you think *that*?' The phone rang again and Macon woke up. There was a thud of disappointment somewhere inside his rib cage. He understood why people said hearts 'sank'.

In slow motion, he reached for the receiver. 'Yes,' he said.

'Macon! Welcome back!'

It was Julian Edge, Macon's boss, his usual loud and sprightly self even this early in the morning. 'Oh,' Macon said.

'How was the trip?'

'It was okay.'

'You just get in last night?'

'Yes.'

'Find any super new places?'

'Well, "super" would be putting it a bit strongly.'

'So now I guess you start writing it up.'

Macon said nothing.

'Just when do you figure to bring me a manuscript?' Julian asked.

'I don't know,' Macon said.

'Soon, do you figure?'

'I don't know.'

There was a pause.

'I guess I woke you,' Julian said.

'Yes.'

'Macon Leary in bed,' Julian said. He made it sound like the title of something. Julian was younger than Macon and brasher, breezier, not a serious man. He seemed to enjoy pretending that Macon was some kind of character. 'So anyway, can I expect it by the end of the month?'

'No,' Macon said.

'Why not?'

'I'm not organized.'

'Not organized! What's to organize? All you have to do is retype your old one, basically.'

'There's a lot more to it than that,' Macon said.

'Look. ... Here it is the third of August. I want this thing on the stands by October. That means I'd need your manuscript by August thirty-first.'

'I can't do it,' Macon said.

In fact, it amazed him he'd found the strength to carry on this conversation.

'August thirty-first, Macon. That's four full weeks away.'

'It's not enough,' Macon said.

'Not enough,' Julian said. 'Well. All right, then: mid-September. It's going to knock a good many things out of whack, but I'll give you till mid-September. How's that?'

> **Notes** [Some of the words and expressions are dealt with in *Working with the text*.]
>
> *Macon* (line 1): (rhymes with *taken*)
> *camp* (line 2): an outdoor holiday for young people in the USA
> *cracked* (line 3): broke, changed tone
> *disappointment* (line 5): a feeling of sadness that you did not expect
> *rib cage* (line 5): the bones around your chest
> *sprightly* (line 9): cheerful
> *super* (line 15): (informal) wonderful, very good
>
> *putting it a bit strongly* (line 16): saying that something is better than it is
> *guess* (line 17): (American) suppose
> *figure* (line 19): (American) plan, intend
> *manuscript* (line 19): first written or typed copy (of the new book)
> *brasher* (line 27): noisier, louder
> *breezier* (line 27): more light-hearted
> *on the stands* (line 36): (here) on sale to the public
> *amazed* (line 39): greatly surprised
> *knock ... out of whack* (line 42): (American) push (other projects) out of the way

Working with the text

Do you like the text? Why or why not?

A Answer the questions.

1. Why is Macon disappointed when he wakes up?
2. What is most of the phone conversation about?
3. What is today's date, according to Julian?
4. What is Julian's first suggested date for handing in the manuscript?

B The phrases on the left (1–4) are from the text. Find them, then match them to their approximate meanings (a–d).

1. a thud of disappointment
2. in slow motion
3. some kind of character
4. carry on this conversation

a. an unusual sort of person
b. a heavy feeling of unexpected sadness
c. go on talking
d. extremely slowly

C Reading between the lines

1. Why does Macon dream of Ethan? How does he feel about his son's death? Find a phrase or sentence in the text which tells you how he feels.
2. Why do you think Julian phones Macon – to welcome him back from his trip or to find out when the manuscript will be ready?
3. Why do you think Julian likes 'pretending that Macon (is) some kind of character'? Is this a gentle way of laughing at Macon, or is it more unpleasant than that? How do you think Julian feels about Macon? How do you know?

4. How different are the two men? From your reading of the text, decide which adjectives are most suitable for Macon and which for Julian. Write M for Macon and J for Julian.

> carefree   quiet   energetic   cheerful
> slow-moving   businesslike   enthusiastic

D Discussion

1. Why do you think Macon is so tired and depressed? Is it because of his son's recent death or the fact that Sarah has left him? Or is it simply that he is tired after his trip to England, or perhaps bored with his writing? What do *you* do if you feel miserable, and someone phones you, wanting to have a lively conversation?
2. Why do Julian and Macon have such different ideas about the amount of work to do on a manuscript? Who do you think is right?
3. Would it be a good idea for Macon to talk to Julian about his feelings of sadness? What would *you* do in Macon's situation?

E Prediction

What do you think happens next? Choose **a**, **b**, or **c** to complete the sentences.

1. Sarah ...

   a. returns to Macon.
   b. decides to live alone.
   c. goes on several long journeys.

The Accidental Tourist

2 Macon …

    a finishes his manuscript on time.
    b gives up work completely.
    c finds a new girlfriend.

3 Julian …

    a marries Macon's sister.
    b finds a writer to replace Macon.
    c has a wonderful new idea for a book.

Language work

A '… can I expect it by the end of the month?' (line 28). Match the expressions with *by* (1–5) with their approximate meanings (a–e).

1 by car   a alone, not with anyone else
2 by accident   b not during the daytime
3 by himself   c not with cash or credit card
4 by night   d without intending to
5 by cheque   e driving

Now use these expressions with *by* in your own sentences: *by bike, by credit card, by tomorrow*.

B 'All you have to do is retype your old one' (line 33). *All you have to do is* means there is just one thing you need to do. Rewrite these sentences, starting with *All you have to do is*.

1 You just need to press the green button.
2 It's simple – just type your name in.
3 You only have to renew your passport.
4 We only need some vegetables. Can you buy them on your way here?
5 There's no problem – just ring the garage and they'll send someone to repair the car.

Now think of your own sentence using *All you have to do is …*

C Collocations are words that go together. 'The phone rang again' (line 4). *Phone* often goes with *rang*. Match the nouns (1–6) to the verbs (a–f) which they go with best in these sentences.

1 A strong wind   a grew fast in the field.
2 Trees   b crashed onto the beach.
3 The sun   c blew through the streets.
4 Rain   d shone brightly all day.
5 The grass   e shook in the storm.
6 Waves   f poured down from the sky.

Now make up a very short story, using three of these collocations.

Role play

Student A: You are desperately trying to finish a homework assignment for school/college. Your teacher/tutor (Student B) is asking you when it will be ready. You need more time, so try to persuade him or her to allow you an extra month. Think up a really good excuse!

Student B: You think your student (Student A) has been rather lazy. You don't want to allow any more time, because that will cause trouble with all the other students. But you don't want to be too hard on him or her, if there is a real problem. So you listen politely, and then decide on a new date when the homework assignment *must* be handed in.

Writing

You are visiting a foreign city and feeling homesick. Write a postcard (35–45 words) to an English friend of yours. In your card, say:

- why you are there
- what sightseeing you have done
- how you are feeling.

11 SEBASTIAN FAULKS
1953–

Sebastian Faulks was born in Newbury, Berkshire, England. After finishing his studies at Cambridge University, he became a journalist. He was the first literary editor of *The Independent* and became deputy editor of *The Independent on Sunday*, but he left in 1991 to concentrate on writing. His first novel, *A Trick of the Light*, was published in 1984, and several others have followed. *Birdsong* (1993) became a best-seller, and *Charlotte Gray* (1998) was made into a film, starring Cate Blanchett. He continues to write fiction, and to contribute articles and reviews to various newspapers and magazines.

Sebastian Faulks is a Fellow of the Royal Society of Literature and was awarded the CBE (Commander of the Order of the British Empire) in 2002. He lives in London, England, with his wife and three children.

Other works by Sebastian Faulks: (novels) *A Trick of the Light, The Girl at the Lion d'Or, Charlotte Gray, On Green Dolphin Street*; (non-fiction) *The Fatal Englishman: Three Short Lives*.

Birdsong

This is the story of a young Englishman, Stephen Wraysford, and his terrible experiences fighting in northern France during the First World War. Stephen and another man, Jack Firebrace, are caught in an explosion in a tunnel which is part of the trench system between the British and the German lines. Three German soldiers are sent down into the tunnel to investigate the explosion. They find the brother of one of them, Joseph Levi, lying there dead. Now they have discovered Stephen, who is injured, and Jack, who by now is dead.

Before you read

Why do you think the author chose the title *Birdsong*? Tick (✔) as many as you like.

a Birds go on singing even if there is a war on.
b Birds need freedom to sing, and people fight wars to be free.
c Only when the fighting is over is it quiet enough to hear birds singing again.

Now read the text up to 'He laid his head against Levi's chest and sobbed.' (line 26).

Think about these questions as you read. Is the text …

… exciting?   … funny?   … difficult?   … scary?   … sad?   … interesting?

Birdsong

They helped Stephen to the bottom of the rope and gave him water. They lifted him up, and Levi walked with his arm round him to the end of the tunnel while Lamm and Kroger went back into the darkness to bring out the body of Jack Firebrace.

Levi guided Stephen's slow steps up the incline towards the light. They had to cover their eyes against the powerful rays of the sun. Eventually they came up into the air of the German trench. Levi helped Stephen over the step.

Stephen breathed deeply again and again. He looked at the blue and distant sky, feathered with irregular clouds. He sat down ... and held his head in his hands.

They could hear the sound of birds. The trench was empty.

Levi climbed on to the parapet and raised a pair of binoculars. The British trench was deserted. He looked behind the German lines, but could see nothing in front of the horizon, five miles distant. The dam had broken, the German army had been swept away.

He came down into the trench and sat next to Stephen. Neither man spoke. Each listened to the heavenly quietness.

Stephen eventually turned his face up to Levi. 'Is it over?' he said in English.

'Yes,' said Levi, also in English. 'It is finished.'

Stephen looked down to the floor of the German trench. He could not grasp what had happened. Four years that had lasted so long it seemed that time had stopped. All the men he had seen killed, their bodies, their wounds. Michael Weir. His pale face emerging from his burrow underground. Byrne like a headless crow. The tens of thousands who had gone down with him that summer morning.

He did not know what to do. He did not know how to reclaim his life.

He felt his lower lip begin to tremble and the hot tears filling his eyes. He laid his head against Levi's chest and sobbed.

They brought up Jack's body and, when the men had rested, they dug a grave for him and Joseph Levi. They made it a joint grave, because the war was over. Stephen said a prayer for Jack, and Levi for his brother. They picked flowers and threw them on the grave. All four of them were weeping.

Then Lamm went looking in the dugouts and came back with water and tins of food. They ate in the open air. Then they went back into the dugout and slept.

The next day Stephen said he would have to rejoin his battalion. He shook hands with Kroger and Lamm, and then with Levi. ...

Levi would not let him go. He made him promise to write when he was back in England. He took the buckle from his belt and gave it to him as a souvenir. *Gott mit uns*. Stephen gave him the knife with the single blade. They embraced again and clung on to each other.

Then Stephen climbed the ladder, over the top, into no man's land. No hurricane of bullets met him, no tearing metal kiss.

He felt the dry, turned earth beneath his boots as he picked his way back towards the British lines. A lark was singing in the unharmed air above him. His body and his mind were tired beyond speech and beyond repair, but nothing could check the low exultation of his soul.

Notes

tunnel (line 2): underground walkway connecting trenches
incline (line 5): steep slope
trench (line 10): protected position, partly underground, where soldiers can stay for a long time
parapet (line 11): low wall to protect soldiers
binoculars (line 11): special glasses to help people see distant objects
deserted (line 12): completely empty of people
the German lines (line 12): where the German army were when last seen
dam (line 13): (usually) wall to keep water safely in a reservoir
burrow (line 22): underground hole where a rabbit lives
crow (line 22): large black bird
reclaim (line 24): get back something that was lost

sobbed (line 26): cried noisily
grave (line 27): hole in the ground where a dead body is buried
prayer (line 29): words spoken to God
weeping (line 30): crying
dugouts (line 31): underground shelters or huts where soldiers can eat and sleep
battalion (line 33): group of soldiers
buckle (line 36): metal fastener for a belt
Gott mit uns (line 36): (German) God with us
embraced (line 37): hugged each other
no man's land (line 39): land which lies between the two opposing armies
lark (line 42): bird with a beautiful song
exultation (line 44): joy, delight

Working with the text

Do you like the text so far? Why or why not?

A Answer the questions.

1 Why do Lamm and Kroger go back into the dark tunnel?
2 Why do Levi and Stephen have to cover their eyes?
3 Why are both the British and German trenches deserted? What has just happened?
4 How long has the war lasted?
5 How does Stephen feel when he thinks of his dead friends?

B Match the adjectives (1–9) to the nouns (a–i), to make pairs of words from the text. Try to do it from memory, then check with the text.

1	slow	a	morning
2	powerful	b	clouds
3	distant	c	steps
4	irregular	d	tears
5	heavenly	e	crow
6	pale	f	rays
7	headless	g	face
8	summer	h	sky
9	hot	i	quietness

C Reading between the lines

1 Why do you think Stephen holds his head in his hands, after he has come up into the air?
2 What is meant by 'the dam had broken' (line 13)?

3 Who do you think Michael Weir and Byrne are? What do you think happened to them?
4 Why is the word 'burrow' used in line 22?
5 Who do you think 'him' refers to in line 23? What event does this sentence refer to?
6 Why do you think Stephen cries? Give at least two possible reasons.

D Prediction

What do you think happens in the next part of the text? Tick (✔) as many as you like.

a Stephen is very grateful to the Germans for saving his life.
b Stephen returns to the British lines.
c They dig a grave and bury Jack and Joseph.
d They promise never to fight each other's country again.
e Stephen is killed by an accidental shot as he enters no man's land.

Now read to the end of the text.

E Answer the questions.

1 Why do they decide to dig a joint grave?
2 Why are all four of the men weeping?
3 Why does Stephen shake hands with the three Germans?
4 What is Stephen almost expecting, as he climbs the ladder into no man's land?

Birdsong

5 How does the word 'kiss' help to describe 'the hurricane of bullets' (line 39)?
6 How does Stephen feel as he walks back to rejoin the British army, and why?

F Reading between the lines

1 Why doesn't Levi want to let Stephen go?
2 Why do Levi and Stephen exchange presents?
3 Why is the air 'unharmed' (line 42)?

G Match the verbs (1–6) with their objects (a–f), to make parts of sentences from the text. Try to do it from memory, then check with the text.

1 dug   a a prayer for Jack
2 said   b his battalion
3 picked   c a grave for him and Joseph Levi
4 rejoin   d the ladder, over the top
5 shook   e hands with Kroger and Lamm
6 climbed   f flowers and threw them on
                    the grave

H Look at these words, which are all parts of the body. Find the odd one out, the word that does not appear in the text. Try to do it from memory first, then check with the text.

arm	eyes	head	hands	foot
	face	lip	chest	

I Discussion

1 Can you imagine what it would be like to fight in a war? What would be the worst part of it, for you? How do you think you would feel at the end of a four-year war?

2 Are there any ways of preventing future wars? Are there any good reasons for going to war? What would make you want your country to go to war?

Language work

A 'They ate in the open air' (line 32). *Ate* is the irregular past simple form of the verb *eat*. Complete the conversation with the correct past simple form of the verbs in brackets.

Sophie: Atchoo!
Fay: Bless you!
Sophie: Thanks. I think I **1**(catch) a cold last Saturday.
Fay: **2**(Do) you? How **3**(that happen)?
Sophie: **4**(You not hear)? I **5**(fall) into the river!
Fay: Oh no, how awful!
Sophie: It was. Luckily a passer-by **6**(pull) me out. I **7**(have to) run all the way home in my wet clothes.

B 'He could not grasp what had happened' (line 19). This is an example of an indirect question. Put the following indirect questions in the correct order.

1 not he know what could he do did
2 wondered she how wait she should long
3 what understand they saying I didn't were
4 her if could early I asked I leave
5 if there asked was any I information more

Role play

Student A: You haven't seen your friend (Student B) for some time. Now you are chatting to your friend in a café, asking about his or her experience of being stuck in an underground railway tunnel yesterday, when there was a power cut. You know no one was hurt, and everyone came out safely, so you feel you can ask about it without upsetting your friend.

Student B: Tell Student A what happened. You were travelling on the underground railway in the rush hour, when suddenly all the lights went out and the train stopped. Soon you and the other passengers heard the driver making an announcement to explain there had been a power cut. Luckily the first carriage had reached the next station, so all the passengers were asked to walk through the train and get out of the first carriage onto the platform. There were railway guards and police there to make sure everyone was safe. You weren't frightened, but it was still a relief to get up into the open air. Tell your friend how you got home on foot/by taxi/by bus.

12 DODIE SMITH
1896–1990

Dorothy Gladys 'Dodie' Smith was born in Whitefield, Lancashire, England and studied drama at the Royal Academy of Dramatic Art. She started working as an actress, but soon turned to writing plays and became one of the most successful writers of her generation. Her most famous play was *Dear Octopus* (1935), which made her rich enough to own a Rolls-Royce, and was filmed in 1943. Her first novel, *I Capture the Castle*, was written when she lived in the USA during the 1940s and published in 1949; it was always her dream to see the book made into a film, but it was not filmed until 2003. Dodie Smith wrote other novels and some children's books, but she is best known today for her novel *One Hundred and One Dalmatians*; at one time she owned nine Dalmatian dogs herself. The book came out in 1956, and was made first into a Walt Disney cartoon (1961) and then into a film (1996) starring Glenn Close.

Other works by Dodie Smith: (plays) *Autumn Crocus, Dear Octopus*; (children's books) *One Hundred and One Dalmatians, The Midnight Kittens*; (novels) *The Town in Bloom, A Tale of Two Families*.

I Capture the Castle

This novel tells the story of 17-year-old Cassandra Mortmain and her extraordinary family. They are renting an ancient English castle from its American owner. It has damp walls and no heating, and has a separate tower on a small hill nearby. They are extremely poor, because Cassandra's father, an author, has not managed to write a single word since the publication of his first book, which was highly praised by the critics. He spends most of his time reading detective novels. Meanwhile the family cannot pay their bills and have hardly enough food to eat. Cassandra decides that Father must be persuaded to write, in order to provide money for the family to live on. She chooses a moment when her stepmother is away, and puts her plan into action, with her younger brother Thomas's help. She asks her father to come and look at something in the tower; he thinks she means storm damage, and hurries along with her.

Before you read

What do you think Cassandra's plan is? Choose **a**, **b**, **c**, **d** or **e**.

- **a** to invite book critics from London to talk to Father in the tower
- **b** to show Father all the unpaid bills on a desk in the tower
- **c** to ask the bank manager to speak firmly to Father
- **d** to take Father's detective novels away from his room
- **e** to lock Father up until he does some writing

What would *you* do in Cassandra's situation?

Now read to the end of the text.

Think about these questions as you read. Is the text ...

... exciting?   ... funny?   ... difficult?   ... scary?   ... sad?   ... interesting?

'Really, I ought to spend more time in here,' Father said as he followed me up the steps outside the tower. I opened the heavy oak door and stood back for him to pass me. He climbed down the ladder inside and stood blinking his eyes.

'Can't see much yet, after the sunlight,' he called up, peering around. 'Hello, have you been camping-out down here?'

'One of us is going to,' I said – then added quickly: 'Go up the staircase a little way, will you?'

'The crumbling's worse, is it?' He went through the archway and began to make his way up the stairs.

Thomas had already crept from behind the tower. I beckoned and he was beside me in a flash. Together, we dragged the ladder up and flung it down outside.

Father shouted: 'Come and show me what you mean, Cassandra.'

'Don't say anything until he comes back,' whispered Thomas.

Father called again and I still didn't answer. After a few seconds he returned through the archway.

'Couldn't you hear me calling?' he said, looking up at us. 'Hello, Thomas, why haven't you gone to school?' We stared down at him. ...

'What's the matter? Why don't you answer?' he shouted.

I racked my brains to think of the most tactful way of telling him what had happened to him. At last I managed: 'Will you please look round you, Father? It's a sort of surprise.'

We had put the mattress from the four-poster on the old iron bedstead, with blankets and pillows. The most inviting new stationery was spread on the rustic table, with stones to use as paper-weights. We had given him the kitchen arm-chair.

'There are washing arrangements and drinking water in the garderobe,' I called down ... . 'We think you'll have enough light to work by, now we've cleared the ivy from all the lowest arrow-slits – we'll give you a lantern at night, of course. Very good meals will be coming down in a basket – we bought a Thermos...' I couldn't go on – the expression on his face was too much for me. He had just taken in that the ladder wasn't there any more.

'Great God in heaven!' he began – and then sat down on the bed and let out a roar of laughter. He laughed and laughed until I began to fear he would suffocate.

'Oh, Thomas!' I whispered. 'Have we pushed him over to the wrong side of the border-line?'

Father mopped his eyes. 'My dear, dear children!' he said at last. 'Cassandra, are you – what is it, seventeen, eighteen? Or are you eight? Bring that ladder back at once.'

'*You* say something, Thomas,' I whispered.

He cleared his throat and said very slowly and loudly:

'We think you ought to start work, Father – for your own sake far more than for ours. And we think being shut up here may help you to concentrate – and be good for you in other ways. I assure you we've given the matter a lot of thought and are in line with psychoanalysis –'

'Bring back that ladder!' roared Father.

DODIE SMITH

> **Notes** [Some of the words and expressions are dealt with in *Working with the text*.]
>
> *oak* (line 2): long-lasting wood from an English tree called the oak
> *blinking his eyes* (line 3): opening and shutting his eyes quickly
> *peering* (line 4): looking
> *camping-out* (line 5): (here) sleeping and eating in the tower
> *crumbling* (line 8): (the tower walls are) breaking into small pieces
> *tactful* (line 19): kind, careful not to hurt or shock someone
> *four-poster* (line 22): old-fashioned bed with hanging curtains around it
>
> *iron bedstead* (line 22): metal bed frame
> *rustic* (line 23): simply made
> *garderobe* (line 25): (old-fashioned) wardrobe, a cupboard for clothes
> *ivy* (line 26): thick green climbing plant
> *arrow-slits* (line 27): narrow windows in a castle for the defenders to shoot through
> *Thermos* (line 28): container for keeping food and drinks warm
> *roar* (line 31): loud shout
> *suffocate* (line 32): die because you can't breathe properly
> *mopped* (line 35): wiped, dried
> *psychoanalysis* (line 42): a way of finding out people's deepest thoughts

Working with the text

Do you like the text? Why or why not?

A The words and phrases on the left (1–8) are from the text. Find them, then match them with their approximate meanings (a–h).

1	tower	a	extremely fast
2	beckoned	b	paper to write on
3	in a flash	c	pulled (something heavy)
4	dragged	d	threw
5	flung	e	thought very hard
6	whispered	f	called (him) forward with my hand
7	racked my brains	g	a large stone structure often built onto a castle
8	stationery	h	spoke very quietly

B Answer the questions.

1 Where do the steps lead to?
2 What is the ladder used for?
3 Where is the staircase?
4 Who removes the ladder from inside the tower?
5 Why is Father surprised to see Thomas?
6 What have Cassandra and Thomas put in the tower?
7 Why are Cassandra and Thomas holding Father a prisoner in the tower?

C Reading between the lines

1 Why does Father think Cassandra asked him to go into the tower?
2 Why does Father think someone has been 'camping-out' in the tower?
3 What does Cassandra mean when she says, 'One of us is going to' (line 6)?
4 What does Cassandra mean when she says, 'Have we pushed him over to the wrong side of the border-line?' (line 33)?
5 How does Father react …
   a when he first realises that he can't climb out of the tower?
   b when he hears Thomas's explanation?

D Find the correct word from the text to complete the sentences about the story.

1 There is a heavy _____ door at the top of the steps outside the tower.
2 You get into the tower by climbing down the _____ inside.
3 Father is worried that the old stones of the tower are _____.
4 The bed in the tower has a _____, with blankets and pillows on it.
5 At night Father can work by the light of a _____.
6 Food will be kept warm in a _____ for him.

55

I Capture the Castle

E What exactly is Cassandra's plan? Put the sentences in the correct order.

  a Don't let Father out until he produces some writing.
  b Remove the ladder from the tower, so Father can't escape.
  c Make Father think there is possible storm damage in the tower.
  d Send good food down to Father in a basket.
  e Get Father to climb down the ladder inside the tower.

F Discussion

  1 What do you think of Cassandra's plan? Is it a good idea to make someone do something by locking them up until they do it?
  2 Why do you think Father hasn't written anything since the success of his first book?

G Prediction

  1 What do you think happens next? Choose **a**, **b**, **c** or **d**.

   a Mrs Mortmain returns unexpectedly and lets her husband out of the tower.
   b Father is very angry with Cassandra and Thomas when he gets out.
   c The plan works, and Father starts writing.
   d Father becomes ill in the tower, and has to go to hospital.

  2 What do you think happens to Cassandra in the end? Choose **a**, **b**, **c** or **d**.

   a She becomes a successful writer herself.
   b She moves into a small, modern, comfortable town house.
   c She falls in love with Simon, the owner of the castle.
   d She marries an old schoolfriend.

Language work

A 'One of us is going to' (line 6). Complete the sentences with the correct form of *be going to*.

  1 We _____ meet up at the Italian café later today. Will you be there?
  2 My friend _____ get the information I need tomorrow, I think.
  3 The police _____ make sure that doesn't happen again.
  4 Our neighbours _____ have their whole house redecorated in the spring.
  5 I _____ go to the tourist office first, and then the museum. Are you coming?

B 'Bring that ladder back at once' (line 36). *Bring* is an example of an imperative, a command. Complete the sentences with the correct verb from the box.

hold switch bring sit listen take

  1 Please _____ your mobile phones off now.
  2 _____ us the lunch menu, please.
  3 _____ the door open for me, will you?
  4 Just _____ in the waiting room for a while.
  5 Now you've captured me, _____ me to your leader.
  6 _____ ! That sounds like a blackbird!

Role play

Student A: You and your friend (Student B) are discussing the best ways of doing your homework for school/college. You find it difficult to get started – you usually spend hours getting ready to do it, and then you find there isn't enough time to do the actual homework! You think it's better to spend a whole day at the weekend on it, and get it all done then. That way you leave weekdays free for sporting activities, seeing your friends, and relaxing.

Student B: You know Student A can't do all his or her homework on one day at the weekend – it's just a way of trying to avoid doing the homework during the week! You think everyone needs a system. There should be a fixed time every day for homework – for example, just before or after supper. Tell your friend that preparing to do homework isn't the same as doing it! Think of ways to help Student A get down to homework more quickly, and actually get it done.

13 J.R.R. TOLKIEN
1892–1973

John Ronald Reuel Tolkien was born in Bloemfontein, South Africa, of British parents. He grew up and was educated in England and gained a first-class degree in English at Oxford University. When he returned from fighting in World War I, he worked on *The Oxford English Dictionary*, then joined the English Department at Leeds University. He moved on to Oxford University; during thirty-four years there as Professor of English he wrote many short stories, studies and translations. One of his most popular works is *The Hobbit*, published in 1937 (the word *hobbit* was invented by Tolkien); it is a story about a race of small people, half the height of humans. Hobbits also appear in Tolkien's even better-known work, *The Lord of the Rings*, a story of the fight between the forces of good, headed by Gandalf the wizard, and of evil, led by Sauron, the Dark Lord of Mordor. It was published in three books, *The Fellowship of the Ring*, *The Two Towers* and *The Return of the King*, from 1954 to 1955, and all three books have been filmed.

J.R.R. Tolkien retired as a professor in 1959. He lived quietly in Bournemouth, England, and then Oxford until his death.

Other works by J.R.R. Tolkien: *The Hobbit, The Adventures of Tom Bombadil, The Silmarillion*.

The Fellowship of the Ring

This text comes from the first book of the *Lord of the Rings* trilogy, *The Fellowship of the Ring*, published in 1954. Bilbo Baggins, a hobbit, is going off on a long journey. He does not know if he will return, so he is holding a party for all his friends and neighbours, because he may not see them again. He has decided to give his comfortable house, Bag End, and most of his possessions to his young cousin Frodo. Bilbo wanted to take his magic gold ring with him, but Gandalf the wise wizard has persuaded him to leave it in an envelope for Frodo.

Before you read

1 How do you think Bilbo got the magic ring? Choose **a**, **b**, **c** or **d**.

   a He found it lying on the ground.
   b His grandfather gave it to him.
   c He stole it from the Dark Lord.
   d He won it by fighting its owner.

2 What do you think the magic ring can do? Choose **a**, **b**, **c** or **d**.

   a produce food and drink out of the air
   b make its wearer invisible
   c carry its wearer to a different country
   d turn things into gold

3 Who do you think 'The Lord of the Rings' is? Choose **a**, **b** or **c**.

   a Gandalf the wizard   **b** Sauron of Mordor   **c** Frodo Baggins

Now read to the end of the text.

Think about these questions as you read. Is the text ...

... exciting?   ... funny?   ... difficult?   ... scary?   ... sad?   ... interesting?

It was a fine night, and the black sky was dotted with stars. Bilbo looked up, sniffing the air. 'What fun! What fun to be off again, off on the Road with dwarves! This is what I have really been longing for, for years! Good-bye!' he said, looking at his old home and bowing to the door. 'Good-bye, Gandalf!'

'Good-bye, for the present, Bilbo. Take care of yourself! You are old enough, and perhaps wise enough.'

'Take care! I don't care. Don't you worry about me! I am as happy now as I have ever been, and that is saying a great deal. But the time has come. I am being swept off my feet at last,' he added, and then in a low voice, as if to himself, he sang softly in the dark:

> *The Road goes ever on and on*
>   *Down from the door where it began.*
> *Now far ahead the Road has gone,*
>   *And I must follow, if I can,*
> *Pursuing it with eager feet,*
>   *Until it joins some larger way*
> *Where many paths and errands meet.*
>   *And whither then? I cannot say.*

He paused, silent for a moment. Then without another word he turned away from the lights and voices in the fields and tents, and followed by his three companions went round into his garden, and trotted down the long sloping path. He jumped over a low place in the hedge at the bottom, and took to the meadows, passing into the night like a rustle of wind in the grass.

Gandalf remained for a while staring after him into the darkness. 'Good-bye, my dear Bilbo – until our next meeting!' he said softly and went back indoors.

Frodo came in soon afterwards, and found him sitting in the dark, deep in thought. 'Has he gone?' he asked.

'Yes,' answered Gandalf, 'he has gone at last.'

'I wish – I mean, I hoped until this evening that it was only a joke,' said Frodo. 'But I knew in my heart that he really meant to go. He always used to joke about serious things. I wish I had come back sooner, just to see him off.'

'I think really he preferred slipping off quietly in the end,' said Gandalf. 'Don't be too troubled. He'll be all right – now. He left a packet for you. There it is!'

Frodo took the envelope from the mantelpiece, and glanced at it, but did not open it.

'You'll find his will and all the other documents in there, I think,' said the wizard. 'You are the master of Bag End now. And also, I fancy, you'll find a golden ring.'

'The ring!' exclaimed Frodo. 'Has he left me that? I wonder why. Still, it may be useful.'

'It may, and it may not,' said Gandalf. 'I should not make use of it, if I were you. But keep it secret, and keep it safe! Now I am going to bed.'

J.R.R. TOLKIEN

> **Notes** [Some of the words and expressions are dealt with in *Working with the text*.]
>
> *sniffing* (line 1): smelling
> *on the Road* (line 2): travelling, away from home
> *dwarves* (line 2): (here) small hard-working people; they helped Bilbo prepare for the party and are travelling with him (singular: *dwarf*)
> *bowing* (line 4): bending his head down, to say goodbye
> *for the present* (line 5): for the moment, for now
> *swept off my feet* (line 8): carried away by a strong feeling
> *with eager feet* (line 15): (here) with enthusiasm, wanting to travel
> *errands* (line 17): (here) reasons for leaving home
> *whither* (line 18): (old-fashioned) where to?
>
> *lights and voices in the fields and tents* (line 20): Bilbo's guests were still enjoying the party
> *hedge* (line 22): small bushes and plants growing in a line at the edge of a field or garden
> *took to the meadows* (line 22): went into the fields
> *rustle of wind in the grass* (line 23): the noise the wind makes in the grass
> *see him off* (line 31): say goodbye to him
> *mantelpiece* (line 34): shelf over a fireplace
> *his will* (line 36): document stating who owns Bilbo's house and valuables now that he has gone
> *wizard* (line 36): person who can make things happen by magic
> *master* (line 37): (here) owner
> *fancy* (line 37): (here) think

Working with the text

Do you like the text? Why or why not?

A The words and phrases on the left (1–8) are from the text. Find them, then match them to their approximate meanings (a–h).

1 longing for
2 a great deal
3 pursuing
4 trotted
5 sloping
6 a joke
7 slipping off quietly
8 troubled

a a lot
b walked quickly with short steps
c wanting very much
d going downhill
e leaving unnoticed
f worried
g following
h something funny which isn't true

B Answer the questions.

1 How does Bilbo feel about starting his journey?
2 Who is going with him?
3 Does Bilbo say goodbye to his guests or to Frodo?
4 Who does Bilbo's house belong to, after Bilbo has left?
5 What is Gandalf's advice to Frodo about the ring?

C Complete the sentences with the correct word from the text.

1 Bilbo looks up at the stars, _____ the air, before he starts his journey.
2 Gandalf says goodbye to Bilbo for the _____.
3 During the party Bilbo slips _____ quietly into the night.
4 He leaves an envelope for Frodo on the _____.
5 Frodo is now the _____ of Bag End, and the owner of a gold _____.

D Reading between the lines

1 Is this Bilbo's first journey? How do you know?
2 What is Bilbo 'old enough, and perhaps wise enough' (line 5) to do?
3 Why do you think Bilbo says, 'I don't care' (line 7)?
4 What does Bilbo's song about 'the Road' tell us about his journey?
5 Does Gandalf expect to see Bilbo again? How do you know?
6 How does Frodo feel about Bilbo, and his journey?
7 Did Frodo know that Bilbo had a magic ring? How do you know?

E Discussion

1 Why do you think Bilbo is going on his journey? Do *you* enjoy travelling? Would you like to travel, like Bilbo, without knowing exactly where you were going?
2 Why do you think Bilbo leaves quietly, without saying goodbye to his friends and family? How would *you* say goodbye to your friends, if you were going on a long journey? Is giving a party a good way of saying goodbye?

The Fellowship of the Ring

3 If you were Frodo, would you take Gandalf's advice, and put the ring in a secret, safe place? Or would you tell people about it, and use it? Give your reasons.

F Prediction

1 What do you think happens to Bilbo in the end? Choose **a**, **b** or **c**.

  a He leads a long and happy life without the ring.
  b He returns to take the ring back from Frodo.
  c He and Frodo never see each other again.

2 What do you think happens to Frodo in the end? Tick (✔) as many as you like.

  a He goes on a long and painful journey with the ring.
  b The ring helps him to be happy at Bag End.
  c He helps to destroy the Dark Lord's power.
  d He loses this ring, but finds another.

Language work

A 'He always used to joke about serious things' (line 30). *Used to*, with an infinitive, tells us about someone's past habits. Make five sentences about yourself with *used to*, talking about things which you did at one time, but don't do any more.

For example: *When I was a child, I used to play with my friends in our garden.*

B 'Don't you worry about me!' (line 7). The verb *worry* usually takes the preposition *about*. Other verbs take other prepositions. Match the parts of sentences, and link them with the correct preposition from the box. Use each preposition only once. There is one extra which you don't need.

with	at	for	about	for	in	on

1 You're going too fast – wait
2 We spent a long time talking
3 I was told to ask
4 Shall we go out? It depends
5 I always disagree
6 Why is he laughing

a me? What's so funny?
b the weather, doesn't it?
c me!
d Tom – his ideas are crazy!
e Angela's problems.
f the manager – is he in?

Role play

Student A: A distant relative has died and left you a valuable old painting in his will. He also left instructions that you should keep it and hang it on your wall. But you don't need a painting, and you *do* need the money you would get from selling it. You feel sure your relative wouldn't mind if you sold the painting. Discuss with your friends (Students B and C) what you should do.

Student B: You can't believe Student A is thinking of selling the painting. Your friend should keep it and pass it on to his or her children, as a family possession. Try to persuade Student A to agree with you.

Student C: You are surprised that Student A hasn't already sold the painting. Why keep something that is no use? The money would be far more useful. Encourage Student A to go ahead with the plan to sell the painting.

Writing

Write a short story (about 100 words) for your class magazine. It must have the title **The Queen's Gold**. Include any of the following:

the Dark Lord
a magic hat
an underground passage
a beautiful princess
the White Queen
a castle on a hill

three black horses
a young farmer
a wise wizard
a talking mouse
a secret map
a room full of gold

14 GRAHAM GREENE
1904–1991

(Henry) Graham Greene was born in Berkhamsted, Hertfordshire, England. He was educated at a school where his father was headmaster, but was unhappy there and ran away. After studying at Oxford University, where he published a book of poetry, he worked for three years as an editor on *The Times,* writing novels in his spare time. In 1927 he married and became a Roman Catholic. He moved to *The Spectator* as film critic and then literary editor. He had already travelled to Liberia and Mexico, but in 1940 he started working for the Foreign Office and was sent to Sierra Leone. This experience produced what some consider his finest novel, *The Heart of the Matter*, set in West Africa. *Our Man in Havana* was published in 1958. He continued to travel and to write until his death.

Graham Greene was a superb storyteller, good at describing the atmosphere of the exotic places he visited. Apart from his novels, he also wrote many short stories, four travel books, six plays, three books about his own life, and four children's books. Several of his novels have been filmed, for example, *The Quiet American*, starring Michael Caine. Of these *The Third Man*, directed by Carol Reed in 1949 and starring Orson Welles as Harry Lime, is certainly the most famous.

Other works by Graham Greene: *The Power and the Glory, Stamboul Train, Brighton Rock, The Heart of the Matter, The Third Man, The End of the Affair, The Quiet American, A Burnt-Out Case, The Honorary Consul.*

Our Man in Havana

The story is set in the 1950s in Cuba, before Fidel Castro's revolution. Mr Wormold is a British vacuum-cleaner salesman in Havana. When he is asked to become a British secret agent – 'our man in Havana' – he thinks the extra income will be useful, so he agrees. Because he can find nothing interesting to tell the Foreign Office, he invents the information he puts in his reports to London. The Foreign Office gets very excited about this information and sends a secretary, Beatrice, and a radio operator, Rudy, to help Wormold find out more about Cuban and Russian activities. In this extract Wormold asks Beatrice to get their codebook, so that he can send a cable to London.

Before you read

What equipment do you think a secret agent in the 1950s used? Tick (✔) as many as you like.

- a codebook
- a mobile phone
- a laptop computer
- invisible ink
- a good camera
- an electric kettle
- a hand gun
- notebooks

Now read to the end of the text.

Think about these questions as you read. Is the text …

… exciting?   … funny?   … difficult?   … scary?   … sad?   … interesting?

'It's in the safe. What's the combination? Your birthday – that was it, wasn't it? December 6?'

'I changed it.'

'Your birthday?'

'No, no. The combination, of course.' He added sententiously, 'The fewer who know the combination the better for all of us. Rudy and I are quite sufficient. It's the drill, you know, that counts.' He went into Rudy's room and began to twist the knob – four times to the left, three times thoughtfully to the right. ...

'Go on,' Beatrice said, 'one more turn.'

'This is one nobody could find out. Absolutely secure.'

'What are you waiting for?'

'I must have made a mistake. I shall have to start again.'

'This combination certainly seems secure.'

'Please don't watch. You're fussing me.' Beatrice went and stood with her face to the wall. She said, 'Tell me when I can turn round again.'

'It's very odd. The damn thing must have broken. Get Rudy on the phone.'

'I can't. I don't know where he's staying. He's gone to Varadero beach.'

'Damn!'

'Perhaps if you told me how you remembered the number, if you can call it remembering...'

'It was my great-aunt's telephone number.'

'Where does she live?'

'95 Woodstock Road, Oxford.'

'Why your great-aunt?'

'Why not my great-aunt?'

'I suppose we could put through a directory-enquiry to Oxford.'

'I doubt whether they could help.'

'What's her name?'

'I've forgotten that too.'

'The combination really is secure, isn't it?'

'We always just knew her as great-aunt Kate. Anyway she's been dead for fifteen years and the number may have been changed.'

'I don't see why you chose her number.'

'Don't you have a few numbers that stick in your head all your life for no reason at all?'

'This doesn't seem to have stuck very well.'

'I'll remember it in a moment. It's something like 7, 7, 5, 3, 9.'

'Oh dear, they would have five numbers in Oxford.'

'We could try all the combinations of 77539.'

'Do you know how many there are? Somewhere around six hundred, I'd guess. I hope your cable's not urgent.'

'I'm certain of everything except the 7.'

'That's fine. Which seven? I suppose now we might have to work through about six thousand arrangements. I'm no mathematician.'

> **Notes**
> *safe* (line 1): solid, locked box where you can keep valuable things
> *combination* (line 1): secret numbers needed to open the safe
> *sententiously* (line 5): trying to appear important
> *drill* (line 7): routine, rules
> *secure* (line 10): (here) impossible to guess
> *fussing* (line 14): confusing, worrying
>
> *damn* (line 16): swear word expressing anger or annoyance
> *great-aunt* (line 21): your mother's or father's aunt
> *directory-enquiry* (line 26): phone call to the service that gives people's phone numbers
> *stick* (line 34): stay a long time
> *cable* (line 41): telegram

Working with the text

Do you like the text? Why or why not?

A Answer the questions.

1 Why has Wormold changed the combination of the safe?
2 Why does Beatrice go and stand with her face to the wall?
3 What does Beatrice mean when she says, 'if you can call it remembering' (line 19)?
4 Why is it impossible to find out more about Wormold's great-aunt?
5 Why is it impossible to guess the great-aunt's phone number?

B The verbs on the left (1–5) are from the text. Match them with their objects (a–e). Try to do it from memory, then check with the text.

1 know   a the knob
2 twist   b the number
3 made   c the combination
4 remembered   d a directory-enquiry
5 put through   e a mistake

C Reading between the lines

1 Why do you think Wormold talks about 'the drill' (line 6) to Beatrice? What impression is he trying to give?
2 Why does Wormold want to get in touch with Rudy?

D True or false? Tick (✔) any true sentences and rewrite the false ones.

1 Beatrice is very polite to her boss, Wormold.
2 Beatrice is pleased that the combination of the safe is so secure.
3 Wormold and Beatrice decide to phone Oxford for help.
4 Great-aunt Kate is also a secret agent.
5 Beatrice is impressed with Wormold's efficiency.

E Discussion

1 Do you think Wormold is …

   a dishonest, because he is lying to the Foreign Office?
   b a traitor, because he is giving false information to his country?
   c sensible, because he is making a little extra money, and not hurting anybody?

2 Would you like to be a secret agent? Do you think it would be an exciting life? Or do you think it would be too dangerous?

F Prediction

What do you think happens in the rest of the book? Choose **a**, **b** or **c** to complete the sentences.

1 Wormold …

   a gives up selling vacuum cleaners.
   b has a great career as a spy.
   c becomes extremely rich.

2 The Foreign Office …

   a finds out Wormold is lying.
   b sends more staff to Havana.
   c has Wormold arrested.

3 Beatrice …

   a tells her employers in London the truth.
   b finds another job in Cuba.
   c falls in love with Wormold.

Language work

A 'It was my great-aunt's telephone number' (line 21). The words on the left (1–8) are all to do with the family. Match them with their meanings (a–h).

1 great-aunt
2 cousin
3 niece
4 brother-in-law
5 grandmother
6 nephew
7 uncle
8 parents

a your brother's or sister's daughter
b your father's or mother's mother
c your brother's or sister's son
d your mother's or father's brother
e your father's or mother's aunt
f your husband's or wife's brother
g your mother and father
h your uncle's or aunt's child

B 'That's fine' (line 43). This is an example of sarcasm, when someone means the opposite of what they say. Beatrice means, 'That's awful!' Read the following sentences and underline the sarcastic expression in each one.

1 Oh wonderful! The car's broken down again!
2 That's really great. Now I've lost my door key.
3 More homework to do, for the weekend! Thanks a lot!
4 So, the richest woman in the world has to pay tax now! Poor woman – however will she manage?
5 Another lovely day – it's pouring with rain again!

Now make up two of your own sentences which include some sarcasm.

C Secret agents have to use a code to prevent the enemy from understanding their messages. Here is a secret message of four words, sent by one secret agent to another. Can you crack the code and find out what the message is?

10 – 15, 6, 6, 5 – 2 – 8, 22, 15

Role play

Student A: You are a secret agent, working abroad and sending useful information back to your country. Of course you haven't told any of your friends or family about being a spy, but a close friend of yours (Student B) seems to suspect what you are doing. You have invited Student B to lunch at your flat, and Student B has just discovered your codebook and extremely expensive camera (they were lying on your desk – you forgot to put them away). Think up a good story to explain why you have a codebook and such a good camera. Whatever you do, don't tell your friend the truth – it would put him or her in danger.

Student B: For a long time now you've suspected that Student A is doing strange things in his or her spare time. Ask for an explanation. You want to know what the camera and codebook are for. If you don't get satisfactory answers, you won't feel you can trust Student A, and perhaps it will be the end of your friendship. Perhaps your friend is doing something criminal, and you will have to tell the police.

15 LAURIE LEE
1915–1997

Laurie Lee was born in a small farming village, Slad, in Gloucestershire, in the south-west of England. First he went to the village school at Slad, and later to school in a nearby town, Stroud. When he was nineteen, he decided to see more of the world outside the quiet valley where his family lived, so he walked all the way to London. He wanted to make his fortune there, but only managed to earn a little money by playing his violin and working on a building site. He decided to travel further, and with just a few words of Spanish, went by ship to Spain. He spent a year walking through and exploring Spain, until the Spanish Civil War broke out. During World War II he worked for the Ministry of Information in Britain and made documentary films in Cyprus and India.

Laurie Lee's best works are his descriptions of growing up in the countryside, *Cider with Rosie* (1959), and his experiences in Spain, *As I Walked Out One Midsummer Morning*. He shows us the atmosphere of these places, so that we can see exactly what they were like, all those years ago.

Other works by Laurie Lee: *A Rose for Winter, As I Walked Out One Midsummer Morning, I Can't Stay Long, Two Women*, and five books of poems.

Cider with Rosie

In the year 1919 the moment has arrived for Laurie, or Loll, as he is called by his family, to go to school for the first time. He is four years old, and lives in a tiny village in the countryside, with no shops, or rail or bus connections. The village school is the only place where he can get an education.

Before you read

Can you predict what will happen? Tick (✔) as many as you like. Do you think Laurie will ...

a go alone to school?
b learn a lot at school?
c make some new friends?
d get into trouble?
e hate his first day at school?

Now read to the end of the text.

Think about these questions as you read. Is the text ...

... exciting?   ... funny?   ... difficult?   ... scary?   ... sad?   ... interesting?

Cider with Rosie

The village school at that time provided all the instruction we were likely to ask for. It was a small stone barn divided by a wooden partition into two rooms – The Infants and The Big Ones. There was one dame teacher, and perhaps a young girl assistant. Every child in the valley crowding there, remained till he was fourteen years old, then was presented to the working field or factory with nothing in his head more burdensome than ... a jumbled list of wars, and a dreamy image of the world's geography. It seemed enough to get by with, in any case; and was one up on our poor old grandparents.

This school, when I came to it, was at its peak. Universal education ... had packed it to the walls with pupils. Wild boys and girls from miles around – from the outlying farms and half-hidden hovels way up at the ends of the valley – swept down each day to add to our numbers, bringing with them strange oaths and odours, quaint garments and curious pies. They were my first amazed vision of any world outside the womanly warmth of my family; I didn't expect to survive it for long, and I was confronted with it at the age of four.

The morning came, without any warning, when my sisters surrounded me, wrapped me in scarves, tied up my bootlaces, thrust a cap on my head, and stuffed a baked potato in my pocket.

'What's this?' I said.

'You're starting school today.'

'I ain't, I'm stopping 'ome.'

'Now, come on, Loll. You're a big boy now.'

'I ain't.'

'You are.'

'Boo-hoo.'

They picked me up bodily, kicking and bawling, and carried me up to the road.

'Boys who don't go to school get put into boxes, and turn into rabbits, and get chopped up Sundays.'

I felt this was overdoing it rather, but I said no more after that. I arrived at the school just three feet tall and fatly wrapped in my scarves. The playground roared like a rodeo, and the potato burned through my thigh. Old boots, ragged stockings, torn trousers and skirts, went skating and skidding around me. The rabble closed in; I was encircled ... . Tall girls with frizzled hair, and huge boys with sharp elbows, began to prod me with hideous interest. They plucked at my scarves, spun me round like a top, screwed my nose, and stole my potato.

Notes [Some of the words and expressions are dealt with in *Working with the text*.]

instruction (line 1): teaching, education
barn (line 2): farm building used for keeping animals or their food in
wooden partition (line 2): piece of wood, dividing building into two rooms
dame teacher (line 3): (old-fashioned) elderly lady teacher in a village school
burdensome (line 6): (here) hard to learn or remember
jumbled (line 6): in the wrong order
at its peak (line 9): (here) at its fullest
hovels (line 11): poor, small houses
oaths (line 12): rude words, swear words
odours (line 12): smells
quaint garments (line 12): old-fashioned clothes
pies (line 13): baked dishes of meat or fruit
scarves (line 17): long pieces of cloth to wear round your neck

I ain't (line 21): (ungrammatical) I'm not
'ome (line 21): home
boo-hoo (line 25): a word to represent the noise a child makes when crying
bawling (line 26): shouting or crying loudly
chopped up (line 28): cut into pieces
three feet tall (line 30): about one metre tall
rodeo (line 31): a show where cowboys ride wild horses
thigh (line 31): the upper part of the leg
ragged (line 31): old, with holes in
skating and skidding (line 32): moving around (him) fast
rabble (line 32): a noisy crowd of people who might cause trouble
frizzled (line 33): very tightly curled
prod me (line 34): poke at me with their fingers
hideous (line 34): awful
plucked at (line 34): pulled at
spun me round like a top (line 34): pushed me round like a toy
screwed (line 35): twisted

Working with the text

Do you like the text? Why or why not?

A Answer the questions.

1 Why were there two rooms in the school?
2 How many teachers were there?
3 How many years did most children stay at school?
4 What did the children learn at school?
5 How old was Laurie when he first went to school?
6 What happened to his baked potato?

B The words and phrases on the left (1–7) are from the text. Find them, then match them with their approximate meanings (a–g).

1 get by
2 outlying
3 curious pies
4 without any warning
5 baked potato
6 overdoing it rather
7 encircled

a strange food
b surrounded
c unexpectedly
d a vegetable cooked in the oven
e exaggerating a bit
f manage with a small amount
g distant

C Match the adjectives (1–12) to the nouns (a–l), to make pairs of words from the text. Try to do it from memory, then check with the text.

1 wooden
2 jumbled
3 dreamy
4 half-hidden
5 quaint
6 amazed
7 womanly
8 big
9 ragged
10 torn
11 frizzled
12 sharp

a list
b hovels
c elbows
d trousers
e boy
f warmth
g partition
h hair
i image
j garments
k stockings
l vision

D Reading between the lines

1 What was Laurie's general view of the education he and other village children received?
2 What do you think this means: '(it) was one up on our poor old grandparents' (line 7)?
3 Why was the school 'at its peak' (line 9) just then? Can you explain what 'universal education' is?
4 Why does Laurie call some of the children 'wild boys and girls' (line 10)?

Cider with Rosie

5 Do you think there are any men in Laurie's family? How do you know?
6 What time of year was it? How do you know?
7 How did Laurie feel about going to school that first day, and why?
8 Why did his sisters tell him he could turn into a rabbit and 'get chopped up' (line 27)? Did that have the right effect on Laurie?
9 What happened to Laurie at school? Do you think it made him unhappy, or did he accept it?

E Discussion

1 Why wasn't Laurie told about school in advance? Do you think his mother or sisters should have told him?
2 Should every child go to school? Or is it better for some children to be taught at home?
3 What age should children start school? Is four years old too young, do you think?
4 What is the purpose of school? What do you learn there, and how useful is it for later life?

F Prediction

What do you think happens in the next few days? Choose **a**, **b** or **c**.

a Laurie gets used to school.
b Laurie refuses to go to school any more.
c Laurie's teacher says he is too young for school.

Language work

A Which is the odd one out?

1 trousers skirt winter coat boots jacket
2 elbow mouth nose tooth eye ear
3 skating skidding walking dancing standing
4 isn't doesn't ain't aren't haven't
5 potato tomato carrot bean cheese

B '... then was presented' (line 4). This is an example of the past simple passive. Complete these passive sentences, using the correct form of the verbs in the box.

give win make cut speak keep

1 Shoes are no longer _____ in that town.
2 French is _____ here.
3 The keys are usually _____ in the hall cupboard.
4 In summer the grass is _____ once or twice a week.
5 The race was _____ by a Kenyan athlete.
6 I was _____ a present when I left my job.

C 'You're starting school today' (line 20). This is an example of the present continuous used for the future. Complete these present continuous sentences with the correct form of the verb in brackets.

1 I _____ a party tonight. All my friends _____. (have, come)
2 _____ you _____ your homework this weekend? (do)
3 We _____ the latest Harry Potter film tonight. I've already got the tickets! (see)
4 I _____ my coach ticket to Paris today, and I _____ a French phrasebook tomorrow! (book, buy)
5 My brother _____ my car for me tomorrow. I hope so, anyway. (repair)
6 Michelle _____ at the station at 5 o'clock, and I _____ her there. (arrive, meet)

Think of three of your own sentences, using the present continuous for the future.

Writing

Your English teacher has asked you to write a story (about 100 words). Your story must begin with this sentence:

I felt very nervous on my first day at school.

16 MURRAY BAIL
1941–

Murray Bail was born in Adelaide, Australia. He lived in Bombay, India, from 1968 to 1970 and in London, England, from 1970 to 1974; he kept a writer's diary of his time in London. His first collection of short stories appeared in 1975. His first novel, *Homesickness*, won the Australian National Book Council Award, and his second novel, *Holden's Performance*, won the Victorian Premier's Award for Fiction. His third novel, *Eucalyptus*, won both the 1999 Commonwealth Writers Prize and the Miles Franklin Award, and he is widely regarded as one of the finest modern Australian writers. His short story *Camouflage* was published in 2000 in a collection of three short stories also entitled *Camouflage*.

Murray Bail lives in Sydney, Australia.

Other works by Murray Bail: *Homesickness, Holden's Performance, Eucalyptus.*

Camouflage

It is early in 1943, during World War II. Eric Banerjee is a piano-tuner, who lives with his wife, Lina, and their daughter, in the city of Adelaide, South Australia. He is a quiet, peaceable man, so he is a little shocked to find himself called up by the army to defend his country. He is told to report to an office to be examined by a doctor, and to collect his uniform.

Before you read

Camouflage means a way of hiding or disguising something so that it looks like its surroundings. What do you think camouflage has to do with the story? Tick (✔) as many as you like.

a Banerjee finds an animal which can make itself look like its surroundings.
b Banerjee prefers not to be noticed by people.
c Banerjee has to help camouflage some army buildings.
d Banerjee has to wear camouflage uniform.

Now read the text up to 'Already he was almost having a good time.' (line 21).

Think about these questions as you read. Is the text …

… exciting?   … funny?   … difficult?   … scary?   … sad?   … interesting?

Camouflage

Eric Banerjee gave his date of birth and next of kin, and was examined by a doctor. Later he was handed a small piece of paper to exchange for a uniform the colour of fresh cow manure, and a pair of stiff black boots with leather laces. At home he put the uniform on again and gave his wife in the kitchen a snappy salute.

It was so unusual she began shouting. 'And now look what you've done!' Their daughter was pointing at him, screwing her face, and crying.

On the last morning Banerjee finished shaving and looked at himself in the mirror.

He tried to imagine what other people would make of his face, especially the many different strangers he was about to meet. In the mirror he couldn't get a clear impression of himself. He tried an earnest look, a canny one, then out-and-out gloom and pessimism, all with the help of the uniform. He didn't bother trying to look fierce. For a moment he wondered how he looked to others – older or younger? He then returned to normal, or what appeared to be normal – he still seemed to be pulling faces.

'I'll be off then,' he said to Lina. 'I can't exactly say, of course, when I'll be back.'

He heard his voice, solemn and stiff, as if these were to be the last words to his wife.

'You're not even sorry you're going,' she had cried the night before.

Now at the moment of departure something already felt missing. At the same time, everything around him – including himself – felt too ordinary. Surely at a moment like this everything should have been different. Turning, he kept giving little waves with his pianist's fingers. Already he was almost having a good time.

At the barracks he was told to stand to attention out in the sun with some other men. Later there was a second, more leisurely inspection where he had to stand in a line, naked. Then an exceptionally thin officer ..., whom Banerjee recognised as his local bank manager, asked some brief questions.

Banerjee's qualifications were not impressive. The officer sighed, as if the war was now well and truly lost, and taking a match winced as he dug around inside his ear. With some disappointment Banerjee thought he might be let off – sent home. But the officer reached for a rubber stamp. Because of his occupation, 'piano-tuner', Banerjee was placed with a small group in the shade, to one side. These were artists, as well as a lecturer in English who sat on the ground clasping his knees, a picture-framer, a librarian as deaf as a post, a signwriter who did shop windows, and others too overweight or too something to hold a rifle.

Over the next few days they marched backwards and forwards, working on drill. They were shown how to look after equipment and when to salute. Nothing much more.

Notes [Some of the words and expressions are dealt with in *Working with the text*.]

next of kin (line 1): (the name of) his nearest relative
was examined (line 1): (his health) was checked; a doctor looked at his body
uniform (line 2): the clothes that soldiers wear, all in the same style
cow manure (line 3): what cows leave on the ground after eating
laces (line 3): strings to tie up his boots
salute (line 4): lifting the right hand to the head; soldiers do it to show respect
screwing her face (line 6): closing her eyes, frowning, looking angry
shaving (line 7): removing the hair from his face
out-and-out gloom (line 10): complete misery or depression
pulling faces (line 14): putting unusual expressions on his face
solemn (line 16): serious
barracks (line 22): buildings used by the army, where soldiers live
stand to attention (line 22): stand up straight
leisurely (line 23): relaxed
naked (line 24): with no clothes on
brief (line 25): short
sighed (line 26): let out his breath unhappily
well and truly (line 27): completely
winced (line 27): moved his face in pain
disappointment (line 28): a feeling of sadness that he is not getting what he hoped for
clasping (line 31): holding tightly
as deaf as a post (line 32): completely deaf, unable to hear anything
rifle (line 33): long gun
drill (line 34): practising marching and obeying orders

Working with the text

A The adjectives on the left (1–7) are from the text. Find them, then match them to their approximate meanings (a–g).

1 stiff
2 snappy
3 unusual
4 earnest
5 canny
6 fierce
7 ordinary

a smart, quick
b serious
c angry, violent
d the same as usual
e clever, knowing
f different from normal
g hard, not soft

B Put these sentences about the first part of the text (up to line 21) in the right order, to show when things happen in the story. Start with **e**.

a He waves to his wife and daughter.
b His wife says, 'You're not even sorry you're going.'
c He wears his uniform at home.
d He tries out different expressions in the mirror.
e Banerjee collects his army uniform.
f He says goodbye to his wife.

C Reading between the lines

1 How does Banerjee's wife feel about him joining the army?
2 Why does he 'pull faces' in the mirror?
3 How does he feel about leaving home? Does his wife realise this?

D Discussion

1 How would you feel if you were Banerjee, going to defend your country in a war? Excited or scared?
2 How would you feel if you were Banerjee's wife? Worried that your husband might die? Or proud of him for fighting for his country?

Now read to the end of the text.

Do you like the text? Why or why not?

E Answer the questions.

1 Does Banerjee have good 'qualifications'?
2 Why is Banerjee 'placed with a small group ... to one side' (line 30)?
3 What are the small group of men taught to do?

F Complete the sentences with the correct word from the text. Try to do it from memory, then check with the text.

1 Banerjee has to _____ to attention with some other men.
2 A very thin officer asks Banerjee some _____ questions.

Camouflage

3 The officer puts a rubber _____ on Banerjee's papers.
4 Some of the men in Banerjee's group cannot _____ a rifle.

G Reading between the lines

1 What impression does the officer give, when he reads Banerjee's qualifications?
2 How does Banerjee feel when he thinks the army will send him home?
3 What kinds of people are in Banerjee's group?

H Prediction

1 What kind of work do you think Banerjee does in the army? Choose **a**, **b** or **c**.

   a He plays the piano to help soldiers relax.
   b He trains other soldiers to march and salute.
   c He paints some army buildings.

2 What do you think happens to Banerjee in the end? Choose **a**, **b** or **c**.

   a He is killed by the enemy.
   b He dies in a plane crash.
   c He saves the lives of his group.

Language work

A 'Then an exceptionally thin officer ..., whom Banerjee recognised as his local bank manager' (line 24). *Whom* is a relative pronoun, linking two parts of a sentence. It refers to a person as the object of a sentence, and is rather formal. Match these parts of sentences, which are all linked by relative pronouns.

1 There'll be trouble for any student
2 There was the same old classroom
3 That was the day
4 I've invited an international expert,
5 On the bus there was an old man,

a whom I recognised as my neighbour.
b who will speak to the staff.
c whose work isn't on my desk by Monday!
d when I found out the truth at last.
e which I remembered from my schooldays.

Now make two sentences of your own, using *who* and *whose*.

B '... a librarian as deaf as a post' (line 32). A *post* is a piece of wood, standing upright in the ground, often holding a gate or a door or a sign. It certainly cannot hear anything! *As deaf as a post* is a well-known expression. Match these parts of other well-known expressions.

1 as dry   a as a hatter
2 as dull   b as the nose on your face
3 as mad   c as pie
4 as plain   d as ditchwater
5 as easy   e as a pancake
6 as flat   f as a bone

Now choose the best expression to describe the things and people in the box.

> a country with no hills
> something that is very clear or obvious
> a very simple thing to do
> a completely crazy person
> a very boring person
> a garden where there hasn't been any rain

Now choose two of the expressions and use them in your own sentences.

Role play

Student A: You are going off on a long and dangerous journey, to the jungles of Borneo/the North Pole/the Gobi desert, and are not sure if you will be coming back. Anything could happen to you. You are saying goodbye to a friend (Student B). Explain why you want to go and what you will be doing. It's a difficult conversation – you must make it clear this could be the last time you see each other.

Student B: You can't believe your friend (Student A) really wants to go off like this. Point out all the possible dangers in the jungle/at the Pole/in the desert, and try to persuade him or her not to go. You get very upset when you hear this may be the last time you see each other.

17 SUSAN HILL
1942–

Susan Elizabeth Hill was born in Scarborough, Yorkshire, England. She wrote her first novel, *The Enclosure*, at the age of fifteen, and it was published in 1961. She went to university in London, studying English at King's College, but has always preferred living in the countryside to living in a town. For a while she worked as a reporter on a local newspaper, and wrote six books between 1968 and 1971; of these, *I'm the King of the Castle* won the 1971 Somerset Maugham Award, *The Albatross and Other Stories* won the 1972 John Llewellyn Rhys Prize, and *The Bird of Night* won the 1972 Whitbread Award. She married in 1975 and has two daughters. She has written radio plays, contributed to arts programmes and published novels and short stories. *The Woman in Black* was published in 1983; it was adapted as a play and has been running at a London theatre since 1988. One of her books for children, *Can It Be True?*, won the 1988 Smarties Award.

Susan Hill now lives in the country, in Gloucestershire, England, with her family.

Other works by Susan Hill: (novels) *A Change for the Better, I'm the King of the Castle, Strange Meeting, Mrs de Winter*; (short stories) *The Albatross and Other Stories, A Bit of Singing and Dancing, The Boy Who Taught the Beekeeper to Read*; (children's book) *Can It Be True?*

The Woman in Black

Arthur Kipps, the young man who is telling the story, is a lawyer in London. One of his firm's clients, Mrs Drablow, has just died, and Arthur is sent to attend her funeral in a small town in the north-east of England. At the funeral he sees a thin, ill-looking woman wearing old-fashioned black clothes, but the townspeople seem strangely unwilling to talk about her. Arthur has to go through Mrs Drablow's papers, and decides to stay in her empty house for a night or two, to get on with the work. Eel Marsh House is a long way from any other houses, and at high tide it is cut off from the land around it, when the sea rushes in to cover the road leading to it. To make himself feel less alone, Arthur has borrowed a small dog called Spider from a friend.

Arthur has gone to bed and slept deeply for a short time. Suddenly he wakes up ...

Before you read

What do you think Arthur is going to find? Tick (✔) as many as you like.

a a ghost in the house
b someone stealing Mrs Drablow's silver
c a dead body in a cupboard
d wind blowing through a broken window
e the kitchen on fire
f a locked door to a bedroom

Now read to the end of the text.

Think about these questions as you read. Is the text ...

... exciting?   ... funny?   ... difficult?   ... scary?   ... sad?   ... interesting?

I saw that it was quite dark but once my eyes were fully focused I saw the moonlight coming in through the window, for I had left the rather heavy, thick-looking curtains undrawn and the window slightly ajar. The moon fell upon the embroidered counterpane and on the dark wood of wardrobe and chest and mirror with a cold but rather beautiful light. ...

At first, all seemed very quiet, very still, and I wondered why I had awoken. Then, with a missed heart-beat, I realized that Spider was up and standing at the door. Every hair of her body was on end, her ears were pricked, her tail erect, the whole of her tense, as if ready to spring. And she was emitting a soft, low growl from deep in her throat. I sat up paralysed, frozen, in the bed, conscious only of the dog and of the prickling of my own skin and of what suddenly seemed a different kind of silence, ominous and dreadful. And then, from somewhere within the depths of the house – but somewhere not very far from the room in which I was – I heard a noise. It was a faint noise, and, strain my ears as I might, I could not make out exactly what it was. It was a sound like a regular yet intermittent bump or rumble. Nothing else happened. There were no footsteps, no creaking floorboards, the air was absolutely still, the wind did not moan through the casement. Only the muffled noise went on and the dog continued to stand, bristling at the door, now putting her nose to the gap at the bottom and snuffling along, now taking a pace backwards, head cocked and, like me, listening, listening. And, every so often, she growled again.

In the end, I suppose because nothing else happened and because I did have the dog to take with me, I managed to get out of bed, though I was shaken and my heart beat uncomfortably fast within me. But it took some time for me to find sufficient reserves of courage to enable me to open the bedroom door and stand out in the dark corridor. ...

After a while, I heard the odd sound again. It seemed to be coming from along the passage to my left, at the far end. But it was still quite impossible to identify. Very cautiously, listening, hardly breathing, I ventured a few steps in that direction. Spider went ahead of me. The passage led only to three other bedrooms on either side and, one by one, regaining my nerve as I went, I opened them and looked inside each one. Nothing, only heavy old furniture and empty unmade beds and, in the rooms at the back of the house, moonlight. Down below me on the ground floor of the house, silence, a seething, blanketing, almost tangible silence, and a musty darkness, thick as felt.

And then I reached the door at the very end of the passage. Spider was there before me and her body, as she sniffed beneath it, went rigid, her growling grew louder.

.....

This was the door without a keyhole, which I had been unable to open on my first visit to Eel Marsh House. I had no idea what was beyond it. Except the sound. It was coming from within that room.

Notes [Some of the words and expressions are dealt with in *Working with the text*.]

slightly ajar (line 3): open a little way
counterpane (line 4): (old-fashioned) covering for a bed, to keep it free of dust
Every hair of her body was on end (line 7): all her hair was standing up
her ears were pricked (line 8): she was listening carefully, with her ears up
spring (line 9): jump to the attack
emitting (line 9): sending out
growl (line 9): the sound a dog makes when afraid or angry
prickling of my own skin (line 11): (here) a stinging, burning feeling on my skin
ominous (line 12): as if something very bad is going to happen
strain my ears as I might (line 14): however hard I tried to hear
bump or rumble (line 15): a noise of something heavy on the floor
creaking (line 16): noisy
moan (line 17): make a low noise
casement (line 17): window
muffled (line 17): not clear, faint
bristling (18): ready to attack
snuffling along (line 19): moving along to sniff or smell something
cocked (line 19): (here) on one side, to listen better
sufficient reserves of courage (line 23): enough bravery (that I didn't know I had)
corridor (line 25): passage in a house, leading to bedrooms
ventured (line 28): dared to take
regaining my nerve (line 30): feeling more confident than before
unmade beds (line 31): beds with no sheets or blankets
seething (line 33): (here) threatening
felt (line 34): thick, soft material
rigid (line 36): hard, unmoving

Working with the text

Do you like the text? Why or why not?

A The adjectives on the left (1–8) are from the text. Find them, then match them with their approximate meanings (a–h).

1	focused	a	stale-smelling
2	tense	b	happening on and off
3	paralysed	c	wrapping round everything
4	faint	d	able to see clearly
5	intermittent	e	something you can touch
6	blanketing	f	with tight muscles
7	tangible	g	quiet, difficult to hear
8	musty	h	unable to move

B True or false? Tick (✔) any true sentences and rewrite the false ones.

1 Sunlight is coming in through the window.
2 The window is tightly shut.
3 Arthur knows at once why he has woken up.
4 Spider knows that something is wrong.
5 The faint noise sounds a long way away.
6 Arthur gets up and goes straight into the corridor.
7 Arthur checks three other bedrooms.
8 The door at the end of the passage is open.

C Reading between the lines

1 Why does Arthur's heart miss a beat?
2 Why is the silence 'ominous and dreadful' (line 12)?
3 Why does Spider growl, again and again?
4 What makes Arthur brave enough to get out of bed?
5 How does he feel as he opens his bedroom door?
6 Why does Spider growl more loudly by the door at the end of the passage?

D Match the adjectives (1–8) to the nouns (a–h), to make phrases from the text. Try to do it from memory, then check with the text.

1	rather heavy, thick-looking	a	wood
2	embroidered	b	beds
3	dark	c	light
4	cold but rather beautiful	d	counterpane
5	soft, low	e	silence
6	regular yet intermittent	f	curtains
7	empty unmade	g	bump or rumble
8	almost tangible	h	growl

E Discussion

1 Do you understand how frightened Arthur is?
2 Do you believe in ghosts? Why or why not? Have you ever seen a ghost? Or do you know someone who has?

The Woman in Black

F Prediction

What do you think happens next? Choose **a**, **b**, **c** or **d**.

a Spider calms down, and Arthur goes back to bed.
b The door opens, and Spider dies of fright.
c Arthur manages to break open the door, and finds the woman in black.
d The woman is black rushes out of the room, and Arthur follows her out of the house.

You will find out what happens at the end of the story when you do Language work C.

Language work

A 'The passage led only to three other bedrooms' (line 29). *Led* is an irregular past simple form. Complete the paragraph about the story by putting a suitable verb in each space.

Arthur slept for a while, but suddenly something **1**_____ him up. He **2**_____ up in bed, and **3**_____ a noise. Although he **4**_____ very scared, he **5**_____ out of bed and **6**_____ a few steps into the corridor. Very cautiously, he **7**_____ a look in some other bedrooms, but he **8**_____ nothing strange there. Finally he **9**_____ to the door without a keyhole. He **10**_____ that the sound was coming from that room.

B 'The moon fell ... on the dark wood of wardrobe and chest and mirror' (line 3). *Wardrobe* and *chest* are pieces of furniture, and you may find several *mirrors* in a house. Say where these things should go in a house or flat, by writing B (bathroom), K (kitchen) or S (sitting room) beside the words. There are five things for each room.

toilet	shower	fireplace
fridge	basin	freezer
cupboard	microwave	cooker
bath	television	piano
dishwasher	stereo	sofa

C 'I sat up ... conscious only of the dog' (line 10). *Of* is the preposition which normally follows *conscious* or *aware*. Other adjectives take different prepositions. Complete these true sentences about the story with the correct preposition.

1 Spider's owner is proud _____ his intelligent little dog, and Arthur becomes quite fond _____ Spider.

2 The woman in black is Mrs Drablow's sister, who comes back to Eel Marsh House as a ghost, because she is angry _____ the death of her son.

3 Arthur is interested _____ the story of the woman's life.

4 Arthur is so shocked _____ his experiences at Eel Marsh House that he becomes ill.

5 Later on, in London, Arthur is very happy _____ his new wife and their baby son.

6 He is not prepared _____ the disaster that happens to him and his family.

7 He is very frightened _____ the woman in black when he sees her again, and soon afterwards, his wife and son are killed in a terrible accident.

Writing

Write a ghost story (about 100 words) for your school magazine. Include any of the following:

a funeral
a windswept hill
a moonlit night
an open grave
a headless man
the sound of a dog growling
a creaking floorboard
a door opens, but there is nobody there
you see someone who nobody else can see

18 JOHN LE CARRÉ
1931–

David John Moore Cornwell was born in Poole, Dorset, England. His mother left the family when he was six, so he was brought up by his father. He studied for a short time at Berne University in Switzerland, did his national service with the British Intelligence Service in Austria, and finally got a first-class degree in modern languages from Oxford University. After trying a number of jobs, he joined the Foreign Office and was sent to the British Embassy in Bonn, then the capital of West Germany. During this time he published his first two novels, *Call for the Dead* and *A Murder of Quality*, using the pen-name John le Carré, because the Foreign Office did not allow their staff to publish under their own names. In 1963 his novel *The Spy Who Came in from the Cold* quickly became a best-seller, winning the British Crime Novel and Somerset Maugham Awards. Now he was able to resign from his job and write full-time. He drew on his own life and experiences to write *A Perfect Spy* (1986), which some consider his finest work. While working for the Foreign Office in Germany, he was also working for MI5, the British counter-intelligence agency, and his books give an insider's view of the world of the spy.

John le Carré lives with his second wife in London, England, and has four sons.

Other works by John le Carré: *Call for the Dead, A Murder of Quality, The Spy Who Came in from the Cold, The Looking Glass War, A Small Town in Germany, Tinker Tailor Soldier Spy, The Honourable Schoolboy, Smiley's People, The Little Drummer Girl, The Russia House, The Secret Pilgrim, The Night Manager, Our Game, The Tailor of Panama, Secret & Secret, The Constant Gardener, Absolute Friends.*

A Perfect Spy

Magnus Pym, diplomat at the British Embassy in Vienna, Austria, and British secret agent, has suddenly disappeared. Jack Brotherhood of the British Intelligence Service has come to Magnus's house to interview his wife Mary and search for clues. Mary was herself trained as a spy, by Jack, when she was younger. Jack's team, Harry, Fergus and Georgie, are searching the house while Jack asks Mary some questions.

Before you read

What do you think the title *A Perfect Spy* means? Tick (✔) as many as you like.

a a spy who never makes a mistake
b someone who thinks spying is more important than anything else in his life
c an intelligence agency's favourite spy
d someone who spies for more than one employer

Now read to the end of the text.

Think about these questions as you read. Is the text …

… exciting?   … funny?   … difficult?   … scary?   … sad?   … interesting?

77

'Why's this drawer empty?' Brotherhood asked.
'I didn't know it was.'
'So what was it full of?'
'Old photographs. Mementoes. Nothing.'
'How long's it been empty?'
'I don't know, Jack. I don't know! Get off my back, will you?'
'Did he put papers in his suitcase?'
'I didn't watch him pack.'
'Did you hear him down here while he was packing?'
'Yes.'

The telephone rang. Mary's hand shot out to take it but Brotherhood was already grasping her wrist. Still holding her, he leaned towards the door and yelled for Harry while the phone went on ringing. It was rising four a.m. already. Who the hell calls at four in the morning except Magnus? Inside herself Mary was praying so loud she hardly heard Brotherhood's shout. The phone kept calling her and she knew now that nothing mattered except Magnus and her family.

'It might be Tom!' she shouted while she struggled. 'Let go, damn you!' ...

Harry must have flown downstairs. She counted two more rings before he was standing in the doorway.

'Trig this call,' Brotherhood ordered, loud and slow. Harry vanished. Brotherhood released Mary's hand. 'Make it very, very long, Mary. Spread it right out. You know how to play those games. Do it.'

She lifted the phone and said, 'Pym residence.'

Nobody answered. Brotherhood was conducting her with his powerful hands, willing her, pressing her to talk. She heard a metallic ping and crammed her hand over the mouthpiece. 'It could be a call code,' she breathed. She held up one finger for one ping. Then a second. Then a third. It was a call code. They had used them in Berlin: two for this, three for that. Private and prearranged between the Joe and base. She opened her eyes to Brotherhood to say what shall I do? He shook his head to say I don't know either.

'Speak,' he mouthed.

Mary drew a deep breath. 'Hullo? Speak up, please.' She took refuge in German. 'This is the residence of Counsellor Magnus Pym of the British Embassy. Who is that? Will you speak, please? Mr Pym is not here at the moment. If you wish to leave a message, you may do so. Otherwise, please call later. Hullo?'

More, Brotherhood was urging. Give me more. She recited her telephone number in German and again in English. The line was open and she could hear a noise like traffic and a noise like scratchy music played at half speed, but no more pings. She repeated the number in English. 'Speak up, please. The line is dreadful. Hullo. Can you hear me? Who's that calling, please? Do – please – speak – up.' Then she couldn't help herself. Her eyes closed and she screamed, 'Magnus, for God's sake say where you are!' But Brotherhood was miles ahead of her. With a lover's knowledge he had felt her outburst coming and clapped his hand over the cradle.

'Too short, sir,' Harry lamented from the doorway.

JOHN LE CARRÉ

> **Notes** [Some of the words and expressions are dealt with in *Working with the text*.]
>
> *Get off my back* (line 6): (informal) stop asking me so many questions
> *shot out* (line 11): reached out fast
> *Tom* (line 17): Magnus's and Mary's son
> *flown* (line 18): (here) run very fast
> *Trig this call* (line 20): (spy talk) find out where the call is coming from
> *conducting* (line 24): waving his hands at her to make her speak
> *a metallic ping* (line 25): a high sound like metal being hit
> *crammed* (line 25): put
>
> *a call code* (line 26): (spy talk) a way of signalling who is calling, or giving a secret message
> *the Joe* (line 28): (spy talk) the secret agent or spy
> *base* (line 28): the spy's home or the intelligence agency's office
> *mouthed* (line 31): silently his mouth made the shape of the word
> *took refuge in German* (line 32): found it easier to speak German
> *Counsellor* (line 33): a diplomatic title
> *scratchy* (line 38): (here) badly recorded
> *clapped his hand over the cradle* (line 43): put his hand on the base of the phone to finish the call

Working with the text

Do you like the text? Why or why not?

A The words on the left (1–6) are from the text. Find them, then match them with their approximate meanings (a–f).

1. mementoes   a suggesting, encouraging
2. struggled   b tried to get away
3. vanished   c said sadly
4. urging   d disappeared, left at once
5. dreadful   e very bad
6. lamented   f objects kept as a reminder of a person or place

B Answer the questions.

1. What time is it?
2. Is anyone except Magnus likely to phone at this time?
3. Why can't Mary answer the phone at once?
4. Does Mary hear the caller speak?
5. Is the call code one that she is using with Magnus?
6. Why does she scream, 'Magnus, for God's sake say where you are!' (line 41)?
7. Does Harry find out where the call is coming from?

C Reading between the lines

1. Why do you think Jack is interested in an empty drawer? What do you think has happened to all the old photos and mementoes that were in it?
2. How does Mary feel when she tells Jack, 'Get off my back, will you?' (line 6), and why?
3. When the phone rings, who do Mary and Jack think is calling? What do you think Mary is praying for?
4. Why does Mary say, 'It might be Tom!' (line 17)?
5. Why does Jack tell Mary to keep the phone call going as long as possible? Why does he say, 'You know how to play those games' (line 21)?
6. The caller is using a call code, so what does that tell us about him or her?
7. How do we know that Mary and Jack had a close relationship in the past?
8. What do Mary and Jack both want?
9. What does Mary *really* fear has happened?

D Here are some jumbled questions from the text. Put the words in the correct order. Do it without looking at the text, then check your answers with the text.

1. empty drawer this why's
2. it of full what so was
3. it how empty long's been
4. suitcase he papers in did his put
5. that is who
6. me you hear can
7. please that calling who's

79

A Perfect Spy

E Match the adjectives (1–7) and nouns (a–g) to make phrases from the text. Try to do it from memory, then check with the text.

1	powerful	a	breath
2	metallic	b	music
3	deep	c	ping
4	British	d	hands
5	telephone	e	Embassy
6	scratchy	f	speed
7	half	g	number

F Discussion

1 Who do you think is making the phone call – Magnus Pym, another spy, a foreign intelligence agency, or someone else?

2 If Magnus is spying for another country as well as for Britain, most people would call him a traitor. Why do you think he would do that – for money, for friendship, for political reasons, or for some other reason?

G Prediction

What do you think happens next? Choose **a**, **b**, **c**, **d** or **e**.

a Magnus, kidnapped by foreign spies, is rescued by the police. He returns to his family.
b Magnus escapes to the foreign country he has been spying for. Mary and Tom join him there.
c Mary discovers that Magnus is with a girlfriend. She forgives him and he comes back to her.
d Magnus knows he is a traitor and kills himself.
e Jack discovers that Magnus has gone mad and is hiding in a friend's house.

Language work

A '... while the phone went on ringing' (line 13). *Go on* is followed by *-ing* (the gerund) when it means *continue*. Some verbs are followed by the infinitive, and some by the *-ing* form; most prepositions are followed by the *-ing* form. Complete the sentences with either the infinitive or the *-ing* form of the verb in brackets.

1 In the end I managed _____ the old lady into her wheelchair. (get)

2 I'm sorry I'm so bad at _____ ! (cook)

3 I really dislike _____ Rosa's children – they're so rude! (look after)

4 The boy finished _____ his story, and gave it to his teacher. (write)

5 I don't feel like _____ for a walk. Let's have a coffee instead. (go)

6 After last year's disaster, we've decided _____ our holiday early this year! (book)

7 I think Lola is too fond of _____ television – she has it on all the time! (watch)

B 'Then she couldn't help herself' (line 40). *Herself* is a reflexive pronoun, and *she couldn't help herself* means *she couldn't stop herself*. Complete these sentences with the correct reflexive pronouns.

> myself   yourself   ourselves
> himself   themselves

1 My brother cut _____ while shaving yesterday.

2 Have you ever tried to teach _____ yoga? It's not easy!

3 When I saw the spider, I told _____ not to be frightened.

4 The boys made _____ go up on stage, although they were both very nervous.

5 We laughed when we saw _____ in the mirror!

Writing

You want to invite a friend of yours to a party tomorrow evening. It is a surprise party for your sister's birthday. Write an e-mail (35–45 words) to your friend. In your e-mail:

- say what time and where the party will be
- tell him or her to keep it secret
- ask him or her to bring a cake.

19 W. Somerset Maugham
1874–1965

William Somerset Maugham was born in Paris, France, and lived there with his British parents. But by the time he was ten, they had both died, so he was sent to live with his uncle in England. Later he studied at Heidelberg University in Germany, and then trained to be a doctor at a large London hospital. For a short time he worked as a doctor in one of the poorest parts of London, and in 1897 he wrote his first novel, *Liza of Lambeth*, about what he saw there.

He decided to be a writer rather than a doctor, and moved back to Paris, where he wrote a number of successful plays. At the beginning of World War I, he became an ambulance driver for the Red Cross in France. Later he became a secret agent, working in Switzerland and Russia. After the war he travelled in the South Pacific, and later in the Far East. Finally in 1928, as a rich and well-known writer, he settled in France, buying a large and beautiful villa on the French Riviera, where many famous people came to visit him and enjoy his hospitality. When World War II broke out, he went to live in the USA, where he stayed from 1940 to 1946. He returned to France after the war and continued writing until his death.

Many of the places Somerset Maugham travelled to and the people he met appear in his stories and novels. His short stories are considered some of the finest in the English language; they often have an unexpected 'twist' at the end.

Other works by Somerset Maugham: *Liza of Lambeth, Of Human Bondage, The Moon and Sixpence, Ashenden, Cakes and Ale, The Razor's Edge,* several plays and many collections of short stories.

The Colonel's Lady

This short story comes from Volume Two of the *Collected Short Stories*, first published in 1951. It is set in the mid-1930s in England. Colonel George Peregrine, a retired military officer, is proud of his name, his family, his appearance, his character and his large country house. He is less proud of his wife, Evie, and, because they have been married for many years, thinks he knows everything about her. But Evie is going to surprise him.

Before you read

How do you think Evie is going to surprise the colonel? Choose **a**, **b**, **c**, **d** or **e**. She's going to tell him that …

- **a** she's expecting a baby.
- **b** she's leaving him for a younger man.
- **c** she has spent a lot of money on new clothes.
- **d** she has bought him a special present.
- **e** she has written a book.

Now read to the end of the text.

Think about these questions as you read. Is the text …

… exciting?   … funny?   … difficult?   … scary?   … sad?   … interesting?

The Colonel's Lady

The Peregrines were having breakfast. Though they were alone and the table was long they sat at opposite ends of it. From the walls George Peregrine's ancestors, painted by the fashionable painters of the day, looked down upon them. The butler brought in the morning post. There were several letters for the colonel, business letters, *The Times*, and a small parcel for his wife Evie. He looked at his letters and then, opening *The Times*, began to read it. They finished breakfast and rose from the table. He noticed that his wife hadn't opened the parcel.

'What's that?' he asked.

'Only some books.'

'Shall I open it for you?'

'If you like.'

He hated to cut string and so with some difficulty untied the knots.

'But they're all the same,' he said when he had unwrapped the parcel. 'What on earth d'you want six copies of the same book for?' He opened one of them. 'Poetry.' Then he looked at the title page. *When Pyramids Decay*, he read, by E. K. Hamilton. Eva Katherine Hamilton: that was his wife's maiden name. He looked at her with smiling surprise. 'Have you written a book, Evie? You are a slyboots.'

'I didn't think it would interest you very much. Would you like a copy?'

'Well, you know poetry isn't much in my line, but – yes, I'd like a copy; I'll read it. I'll take it along to my study. I've got a lot to do this morning.'

He gathered up *The Times*, his letters, and the book, and went out. His study was a large and comfortable room, with a big desk, leather arm-chairs, and what he called 'trophies of the chase' on the walls. On the bookshelves were works of reference, books on farming, gardening, fishing, and shooting ... . At the end of the war he had retired and settled down to the life of a country gentleman in the spacious house, some twenty miles from Sheffield, which one of his forebears had built in the reign of George III. ...

He was a good shot, a golfer, and though now a little over fifty could still play a hard game of tennis. He could describe himself ... as an all-round sportsman.

He had been putting on weight lately, but was still a fine figure of a man; tall, with grey curly hair, only just beginning to grow thin on the crown, frank blue eyes, good features, and a high colour. ... He would have been pleased and at the same time slightly embarrassed if someone had told him he was a jolly good fellow. That was what he wanted to be. He desired no higher praise.

It was hard luck that he had no children. He would have been an excellent father, kindly but strict, and would have brought up his sons as gentlemen's sons should be brought up, sent them to Eton, you know, taught them to fish, shoot, and ride. ...

Evie had been a sad disappointment to him. Of course she was a lady, and she had a bit of money of her own; she managed the house uncommonly well and she was a good hostess. The village people adored her. She had been a pretty little thing when he married her, with a creamy skin, light brown hair, and a trim figure, healthy too, and not a bad tennis player; he couldn't understand why she'd had no children; of course she was faded now, she must be getting on for five and forty.

W. SOMERSET MAUGHAM

Notes [Some of the words and expressions are dealt with in *Working with the text*.]

ancestors (line 2): members of your family who are dead now
butler (line 3): a male servant who usually serves meals and drinks
colonel (line 4): an army officer of high rank
The Times (line 5): a British daily newspaper
string (line 12): long thin material used for tying up parcels
pyramids (line 15): things with a flat bottom and three or four sloping sides that come to a point at the top
decay (line 15): fall into ruins
maiden name (line 16): a woman's name before she is married
slyboots (line 17): (old-fashioned) someone who does something secretly
isn't much in my line (line 19): doesn't interest me
spacious (line 25): large, having a lot of space
forebears (line 26): ancestors
George III (line 27): King of England between 1760 and 1820
putting on weight (line 30): becoming fatter
slightly embarrassed (line 33): (here) a little uncomfortable
a jolly good fellow (line 33): (old-fashioned) a nice man, a good friend
Eton (line 37): the most famous English private school for boys
trim figure (line 41): a good shape, a slim body
faded (line 43): no longer fresh or pretty

Working with the text

Do you like the text? Why or why not?

A The following sentences are all taken from the text. Complete them with the correct word from the pair in brackets. Try to do it from memory first, then check with the text.

1 The Peregrines were having _____. (breakfast/lunch)
2 The butler brought in the morning _____. (tea/post)
3 (The colonel) noticed that his wife hadn't opened the _____. (curtains/parcel)
4 'But they're all the _____,' (the colonel) said. (same/better)
5 (The colonel) looked at her with smiling _____. (eyes/surprise)
6 (Evie asked,) 'Would you like a _____?' (coffee/copy)
7 (The colonel said,) 'I'll take it along to my _____.' (study/secretary)

B True or false? Tick (✔) any true sentences and rewrite the false ones.

1 When they have their meals, the Peregrines sit side by side.
2 There are some letters for the colonel.
3 The colonel knows his wife has written a book.
4 The colonel starts reading his newspaper after leaving the table.
5 The colonel has a large study for his private use.

C The phrases on the left (1–10) are from the text. Find them, then match them with their approximate meanings (a–j).

1 trophies of the chase
2 works of reference
3 a good shot
4 a little over fifty
5 an all-round sportsman
6 a fine figure of a man
7 (having) a high colour
8 hard luck
9 a good hostess
10 getting on for five and forty

a someone who shoots well
b good at all sports
c very unfortunate
d almost forty-five
e a good-looking man
f a woman who entertains guests well
g factual books, like dictionaries
h in his early fifties
i heads of animals which were hunted and killed
j with pink cheeks

The Colonel's Lady

D Imagine you are the colonel. Make a list of Evie's good and bad points, as you think he sees them.

good points	bad points
Example: she's a lady	she hasn't given him any children

Now imagine you are Evie. Make a list of the colonel's good and bad points, as you think she sees them.

good points	bad points
Example: he's a gentleman	he doesn't like poetry

We know that Evie has been 'a sad disappointment' to the colonel, but do you think the colonel has also been a sad disappointment to Evie? Why or why not?

E Discussion

1 How can you describe the colonel's character?
2 What do you think Evie's poetry is about, and what made her start writing? Why did she use her maiden name?

F Prediction

What do you think happens in the rest of the story? Tick (✔) as many as you like. The colonel ...

a is shocked by Evie's poetry.
b discovers that Evie is in love.
c understands Evie better than before.
d and Evie separate.
e and Evie stay together.

Language work

A 'Have you written a book, Evie?' (line 17). This is a question in the present perfect tense. Complete these questions about the story with the correct form of the verb in brackets. Then give a short answer to each question, based on your understanding of the text and your own opinions.

1 Have the Peregrines ever _____ happy together? (be)
2 Has Evie ever _____ a book before? (write)
3 Have the Peregrines _____ any children? (have)
4 Has the colonel ever _____ reading poetry? (enjoy)
5 Has the colonel ever really _____ his wife? (understand)
6 Has the colonel always _____ more about himself than anyone else? (think)

B ' ... she managed the house uncommonly well' (line 39). *Well* is an irregular adverb. It is the adverb form of the adjective *good*. Complete the sentences with the correct adverb form of the adjectives in the box. They are all irregular.

fast   late   hard   good

1 No one cooks as _____ as my mother does. Her food is wonderful!
2 If I can get the taxi driver to drive really _____, I think I'll be able to catch the 5 o'clock train.
3 I pushed _____ on the door, but it still didn't open.
4 I arrived too _____ for the meeting, and my boss was angry with me.

Writing

You have just won a writing competition. Write an e-mail (35–45 words) to a friend of yours about it. In your email, explain:

- what kind of writing it was
- what the prize was
- how you feel about winning.

20 PATRICIA HIGHSMITH
1921–1995

Patricia Highsmith was born in Fort Worth, Texas, USA, but moved to New York with her parents when she was six years old. She edited her school magazine, and at the age of sixteen she decided to become a writer. The director Alfred Hitchcock made a film of her first novel, *Strangers on a Train*; her third novel, *The Talented Mr Ripley* (1956), won the Edgar Allan Poe Scroll, awarded by the Mystery Writers of America. She wrote many books and short stories, and lived for most of her life in Switzerland.

Patricia Highsmith said that she was 'interested in the effect of guilt' on her heroes; she specialised in getting inside the minds of her characters. This is particularly true of *The Talented Mr Ripley*, which is written completely from the point of view of Tom Ripley. He is a young man with no morals, who wants all the things money can buy – expensive clothes, books, furniture and holidays – and is prepared to kill to get them. Two films have been made of the book, one in 1959, starring Alain Delon, and another in 1999, starring Matt Damon, Gwyneth Paltrow and Jude Law. The book was so successful that three more novels about Ripley soon followed; two of them have been filmed.

Other works by Patricia Highsmith: *Deep Water, This Sweet Sickness, The Cry of the Owl, The Glass Cell, Ripley Under Ground, Ripley's Game, Edith's Diary, The Boy Who Followed Ripley, People Who Knock on the Door, Found in the Street,* and seven collections of short stories.

The Talented Mr Ripley

Tom Ripley, living in New York, unemployed and short of money, is contacted by the wealthy Mr Greenleaf, who thinks Tom is a close friend of his son Richard's. Mr Greenleaf asks Tom to go to Italy to find Richard (often called Dickie) and persuade him to return to New York. Tom agrees, as Mr Greenleaf is offering to pay all the expenses, and finds Dickie living in a small Italian village. Tom enjoys Dickie's European lifestyle so much that he wants it for himself, with all the luxuries that Dickie can afford. So he murders Dickie, and drops the body into the sea. He writes a will on Dickie's typewriter, copying Dickie's signature carefully by hand. The will leaves all Dickie's money and possessions to Tom Ripley.

Before you read

1 Who do you think Tom is going to send the will to? Choose **a**, **b**, **c**, **d**, **e** or **f**.

   a his own lawyer
   b an independent lawyer
   c the police
   d Mr Greenleaf's lawyer
   e Mr Greenleaf
   f an old friend of Dickie's

2 What kind of feeling should Tom show in the letter he sends with the will? Tick (✔) as many as you like.

   • sadness • surprise • happiness • anger • sympathy • bitterness

Now read the first text.

Think about these questions as you read. Is the text ...

... exciting?   ... funny?   ... difficult?   ... scary?   ... sad?   ... interesting?

Venice
3 June, 19—

Dear Mr Greenleaf:

While packing a suitcase today, I came across an envelope that Richard gave me in Rome, and which for some unaccountable reason I had forgotten until now. On the envelope was written 'Not to be opened until June' and, as it happens, it is June. The envelope contained Richard's will, and he leaves his income and possessions to me. I am as astounded by this as you probably are, yet from the wording of the will (it is typewritten) he seems to have been in possession of his senses.

I am only bitterly sorry I did not remember having the envelope, because it would have proven much earlier that Dickie intended to take his own life. I put it into a suitcase pocket, and then I forgot it. He gave it to me on the last occasion I saw him, in Rome, when he was so depressed.

On second thought, I am enclosing a photostat copy of the will so that you may see it for yourself. This is the first will I have ever seen in my life and I am absolutely unfamiliar with the usual procedure. What should I do?

Please give my kindest regards to Mrs Greenleaf and realize that I sympathize deeply with you both, and regret the necessity of writing this letter. Please let me hear from you as soon as possible. My next address will be:
    c/o American Express
      Athens, Greece

Most sincerely yours,

Tom Ripley

> **Notes** [Some of the words and expressions are dealt with in *Working with the text*.]
>
> *talented* (in the title of the book): very clever, especially good at certain things
> *unaccountable* (line 5): there seemed to be no reason
> *Richard's will* (line 7): a document explaining who should get Richard's possessions after his death
> *possessions* (line 7): the things someone owns
> *astounded* (line 8): very surprised
> *depressed* (line 13): unhappy, miserable
> *photostat copy* (line 14): photocopy
> *c/o* (line 20): care of (letters can be delivered here)

Working with the text

Do you like the first text? Why or why not?

A The words and phrases on the left (1–7) are from the text. Find them, then match them with their approximate meanings (a–g).

1 came across
2 in possession of his senses
3 take his own life
4 enclosing
5 am absolutely unfamiliar with
6 sympathize deeply with
7 regret the necessity of

a mentally fit, not mad
b have no idea about
c found by chance
d am sorry I have to
e kill himself
f putting in, sending
g am thinking warmly of

B Reading between the lines

1 Why does Tom pretend he has only just found Dickie's will?
2 Why does Tom pretend to be 'astounded' (line 8)?
3 How does the envelope prove 'that Dickie intended to take his own life' (line 11)?
4 Why does Tom pretend that this is the first will he has seen?

C Match the adjectives (1–6) with the nouns (a–f), to make pairs of words from the text. Try to do it from memory, then check with the text.

1 unaccountable
2 second
3 first
4 usual
5 kindest
6 next

a regards
b procedure
c address
d thought(s)
e will
f reason

D Prediction

What do you think happens next? Choose **a**, **b**, **c**, **d** or **e**.

a Mr Greenleaf suspects Tom of killing Dickie and tells the police.
b The police discover Dickie's body and arrest Tom for murder.
c The Greenleafs accept the will as Dickie's, and Tom becomes a very rich man.
d When Tom reaches Athens, he finds a job, so he doesn't need Dickie's money.
e Tom suddenly feels sorry he has killed Dickie, and tells one of Dickie's friends the truth.

The Talented Mr Ripley

The story continues

Tom leaves Italy and sails to Greece. He is extremely nervous when he arrives in Athens and collects his letters from the American Express office. His plan is to move on, to the island of Crete, but he is expecting to be arrested at any minute for Dickie's murder. However, when he opens Mr Greenleaf's reply to his letter about the will, he discovers some surprising news – the Greenleafs believe that their son killed himself, and they accept the will. Their lawyers will now arrange for Tom to receive all of Dickie's money.

Now read the second text, which runs to the end of the book.

Was it a joke? But the Burke-Greenleaf letterpaper in his hand felt authentic – thick and slightly pebbled and the letterhead engraved – and besides, Mr Greenleaf wouldn't joke like this, not in a million years. Tom walked on to the waiting taxi. It was no joke. It was his! Dickie's money and his freedom. ••• He could have a house in Europe and a house in America too, if he chose.

•••••

He tried to imagine landing in Crete – the long island, peaked with the dry, jagged lips of craters, the little bustle of excitement on the pier as his boat moved into the harbour, the small-boy porters, avid for his luggage and his tips, and he would have plenty to tip them with, plenty for everything and everybody. He saw four motionless figures standing on the imaginary pier, the figures of Cretan policemen waiting for him, patiently waiting with folded arms. He grew suddenly tense, and his vision vanished. Was he going to see policemen waiting for him on every pier that he ever approached? In Alexandria? Istanbul? Bombay? Rio? No use thinking about that. He pulled his shoulders back. No use spoiling his trip worrying about imaginary policemen. Even if there *were* policemen on the pier, it wouldn't necessarily mean –

'A donda, a donda?' the taxi driver was saying, trying to speak Italian for him.

'To a hotel, please,' Tom said. 'Il meglio albergo. Il meglio, il meglio!'

> **Notes** *Burke-Greenleaf* (line 24): the name of Mr Greenleaf's company
> *authentic* (line 24): real
> *pebbled* (line 25): bumpy
> *letterhead engraved* (line 25): the company address pre-printed on paper for business letters
> *Crete* (line 29): Greek island which Tom has always wanted to visit
> *peaked* (line 29): with high points
> *jagged* (line 29): rough, not smooth
> *lips of craters* (line 30): edges of deep holes in the earth
> *bustle* (line 30): noisy activity
> *pier* (line 30): a long structure in a harbour where boats can stop and tie up
> *porters* (line 31): people who carry luggage for other people
> *avid* (line 31): keen, greedy
> *tips* (line 31): small amounts of money, e.g. for carrying luggage
> *motionless* (line 32): not moving
> *A donda?* (line 39): the Greek taxi driver is trying to ask 'Where to?' in Italian, because Tom was speaking Italian to him
> *Il meglio albergo* (line 40): (Italian) the best hotel

Working with the text

E Answer the questions.

1 What is Tom's first reaction to Mr Greenleaf's letter?
2 What is Tom's second reaction?
3 Who are the 'four motionless figures' (line 32)?

F Reading between the lines

1 Why do you think Tom is looking forward to visiting Crete?
2 Why does Tom imagine the police will be waiting for him in Crete?
3 Complete Tom's unfinished sentence: 'Even if there *were* policemen on the pier, it wouldn't necessarily mean –' (line 38).
4 How does Tom feel when he says, 'Il meglio albergo' (line 40) to the taxi-driver, and why does he say it?

G Complete the sentences about the second text with words from the text. Try to do it from memory, then check with the text.

1 Tom realises the letter cannot be a _____.
2 He's delighted that he'll get _____ and _____.
3 Tom likes giving large tips to _____.
4 In the end he stops worrying about _____.
5 He asks the _____ to take him to the best hotel in Athens.

H Discussion

1 Why do you think the Greenleafs come to believe their son killed himself? Why do they let Tom have Dickie's money? Think of possible reasons.
2 Do you like Tom or not? Do you feel sorry for him, or admire his cleverness? Or is he simply a hateful criminal?
3 Will Tom always be as happy as he is at the end of the story? What kind of life do you think he will have in future?
4 By the end of the book, Tom seems to have avoided any punishment for murder. He is going to live in freedom, as a rich man. What do you think about this? Is it a good ending or not? If not, what would you like to see happen?

The Talented Mr Ripley

Language work

A 'I came across an envelope' (line 4). *Come across* is a phrasal verb, meaning *find by chance*. Match these common phrasal verbs with their meanings (they may have other meanings as well).

1 break down	a try to find information
2 set off	b collect
3 find out	c become adult
4 grow up	d make progress
5 run out of	e stop working
6 look after	f start a journey
7 turn off	g have no more left
8 call for	h discover
9 get on	i take care of
10 look up	j switch off or stop

Now use two of these phrasal verbs in your own sentences.

B '… so that you may see it for yourself' (line 14). *So that* explains the purpose of an action. Match the parts of sentences, and link them with *so that*.

1 Josie saved some money
2 I'm giving you the facts
3 Ed's doing his homework now
4 Jeff's planting some apple trees
5 Mum's cooking the chicken now

a we can eat it cold later.
b he can go out tonight.
c one day he can eat his own fruit.
d she could buy a sailing boat.
e you can decide for yourself.

C 'He tried to imagine landing in Crete' (line 29). *Imagine* is followed by a gerund, the *-ing* form. Complete the sentences with the *-ing* form of the verbs in the box. There is one extra verb that you don't need.

| drive   do   shake   watch   collect   put |

1 I've always hated _____ horror films.
2 I'm a bit afraid of _____ in heavy traffic.
3 Are you any good at _____ crosswords?
4 Jane's interested in _____ glass bottles.
5 I think I remember _____ the keys in my pocket.

Role play

Student A: You have just heard that an uncle has left you a lot of money in his will. You never cared for him very much, but you were always very polite to him! Now you'll be able to travel round the world, as you've always wanted, and then buy a luxury apartment. You are very excited about your plans. Tell your friend (Student B) about it.

Student B: You are shocked that your friend (Student A) doesn't seem at all sad about the death of his uncle, and is much too interested in the money. Remind your friend how fond of this uncle he or she used to be, and point out that it would be sensible to save some of the money, and not spend it all at once. Secretly, you are a bit envious – you certainly haven't got enough money for a world trip or a luxury apartment!

Writing

This is part of a letter you receive from an English penfriend.

> *So, you see, I can't come on holiday with you this summer. I'm really sorry. Please apologise to your family for me. Perhaps next year?*

Now write a letter (about 100 words), replying to your penfriend.

21 LOUIS DE BERNIÈRES
1954–

Louis de Bernières was born in London, England. He spent four months in the British Army, but left because he decided he believed in peace, not war. He went to live in a village in Colombia, South America, where he worked as an English teacher in the mornings and as a cowboy in the afternoons. A year later he was back in England, where he studied philosophy for a while, and then worked in several short-term jobs; he was a mechanic, a landscape gardener and a teacher. He decided to be a full-time writer, and published his first novel in 1990, *The War of Don Emmanuel's Nether Parts*; it won the Commonwealth Writers Prize, Best First Book 1991. His next novel, *Señor Vivo and the Coca Lord*, won the Commonwealth Writers Prize, Best Book 1992, and in 1993 he was selected as one of the twenty Best of Young British Novelists. In 1992 he visited the Greek island of Cephallonia, and explored it by motorbike with his girlfriend. He went on to write *Captain Corelli's Mandolin* (1994), a story set on Cephallonia, about the power of love and the stupidity of war. The novel became hugely popular and won the Commonwealth Writers Prize, Best Book 1995. It has been made into a successful film, starring Nicolas Cage and Penelope Cruz.

Louis de Bernières lives in London.

Other works by Louis de Bernières: *The War of Don Emmanuel's Nether Parts, Señor Vivo and the Coca Lord, The Troublesome Offspring of Cardinal Guzman.*

Captain Corelli's Mandolin

It is 1941, during World War II, and Captain Antonio Corelli, a young Italian officer, is sent with the invading Italian army to occupy the Greek island of Cephallonia. Dr Iannis and his beautiful daughter Pelagia are forced to let him live in their small village house. He sleeps in Pelagia's bed, and she sleeps on the kitchen floor. He brings a case with him, which he calls Antonia. While they are eating supper together, Dr Iannis is so cold and unfriendly to Corelli that Pelagia almost feels sorry for the young man and, when her father gets up to go for a walk, she starts a conversation with him.

Before you read

How important do you think the mandolin of the title (see *Notes* on page 93) will be in the story? Tick (✔) as many as you like.

- **a** It will bring together two people who love each other.
- **b** It will save a man's life.
- **c** It will prove that music is better than politics.
- **d** Its name will be given to a baby girl.
- **e** Its music will become famous all round the world.

Now read to the end of the text.

Think about these questions as you read. Is the text …

… exciting?   … funny?   … difficult?   … scary?   … sad?   … interesting?

'What is Antonia?' she asked.

He avoided her eyes, 'My mandolin. I am a musician.'

'A musician? In the Army?'

'When I joined, Kyria Pelagia, Army life consisted mainly of being paid for sitting about doing nothing. Plenty of time for practice, you see. I had a plan to become the best mandolin player in Italy, and then I would leave the Army and earn a living. I didn't want to be a café player, I wanted to play Hummel and Conforto and Giuliani. There's not much demand, so you have to be very good.'

'You mean you're a soldier by mistake?' asked Pelagia, who had never heard of any of these composers.

'It was a plan that went wrong; the Duce got some big ideas.' He looked at her wistfully.

'After the war,' she said.

He nodded and smiled, 'After the war.'

'I want to be a doctor,' said Pelagia, who had not even mentioned this idea to her father.

That night, just as she was drifting off to sleep beneath her blankets, she heard a muffled cry, and shortly afterwards the captain appeared in the kitchen, a little wide-eyed, a towel wrapped about his waist. She sat up, clutching the blankets. ...

'Forgive me,' he said, perceiving her alarm, 'but there appears to be an enormous weasel on my bed.'

Pelagia laughed, 'That's not a weasel, that's Psipsina. She is our pet. She always sleeps on my bed.'

'What is it?'

Pelagia could not resist essaying her father's mode of resistance: 'Haven't you heard of Greek cats?'

The captain looked at her suspiciously, shrugged his shoulders, and returned to his room. He approached the pine marten and stroked it on the forehead with a tentative forefinger. It felt very soft and comforting. 'Micino, micino,' he cooed speculatively, and fondled her ears. Psipsina sniffed at the wiggling digit, did not recognise it, surmised that it might be edible, and bit it.

Captain Antonio Corelli snatched his hand away, watched the beads of blood well out of his finger, and fought against the shamingly childish tears that were rising unbidden to his eyes. He attempted by force of will to suppress the mounting sting of the bite, and knew for certain that he had been pierced through to the bone. Never, in all his life, had he felt so unloved. These Greeks. When they said 'ne' it meant 'yes', when they nodded it meant 'no', and the more angry they were, the more they smiled. Even the cats were from another planet, and moreover could have no possible motive for such malice.

He lay abjectly upon the hard cold floor, unable to sleep, until at last Psipsina missed Pelagia, and went off to look for her. He climbed back into the bed and sank gratefully into the mattress.

LOUIS DE BERNIÈRES

> **Notes** [Some of the words and expressions are dealt with in *Working with the text*.]
>
> *mandolin* (line 2): string instrument, similar to the lute
> *Kyria* (line 4): (Greek) usually means *Mrs*, but possibly used here as a sign of respect
> *the Duce* (line 11): the title taken by Benito Mussolini as leader of Fascist Italy (1922–43)
> *wistfully* (line 12): with regret
> *nodded* (line 14): moved his head up and down to agree with her
> *muffled* (line 18): (here) a sound that someone has tried to keep quiet
> *weasel* (line 21): small, reddish-brown wild animal
> *Psipsina* (line 22): Pelagia's pet pine marten, a dark brown animal, looking a little like a wild cat
>
> *essaying* (line 25): (old-fashioned) trying, attempting
> *tentative* (line 28): cautious, trying something very gently
> *micino* (line 29): (Italian) a word used when speaking to a cat
> *cooed* (line 29): a way of speaking lovingly to animals
> *speculatively* (line 29): trying something out
> *fondled* (line 30): patted, stroked
> *surmised* (line 31): assumed, supposed
> *edible* (line 31): eatable
> *well out* (line 32): come out
> *unbidden* (line 34): against his will
> *ne* (line 36): (Greek) yes
> *nodded* (line 37): Greeks have a way of moving their heads up and down to say no
> *abjectly* (line 40): miserably

Working with the text

Do you like the text? Why or why not?

A The phrases on the left (1–8) are from the text. Find them, then match them to their approximate meanings (a–h).

1 avoided her eyes
2 earn a living
3 drifting off
4 a little wide-eyed
5 perceiving her alarm
6 mode of resistance
7 wiggling digit
8 motive for such malice

a reason for being so evil
b looking surprised
c moving finger
d make money from working
e did not look at her
f beginning to go to sleep
g way of making things difficult for the enemy
h noticing she was afraid

B Complete the sentences about the text in your own words.

1 Corelli wanted to become the best mandolin player in Italy, so that he could _____.

2 Corelli's plan did not succeed because _____.

3 Pelagia tries to cheer Corelli up by saying that when the war _____ he can _____.

4 Corelli is surprised to discover _____ on his bed.

5 Psipsina bites his finger because _____.

6 Corelli does not want to cry, but the pain _____.

7 Corelli feels depressed because _____.

8 Corelli does not go back to bed until _____.

C Reading between the lines

Choose the best answer.

1 Why do you think Corelli avoids Pelagia's eyes, in line 2?
   a He is not telling the truth.
   b The doctor made him feel uncomfortable.
   c He can see Pelagia is angry with him.

2 Who or what are Hummel, Conforto and Giuliani?
   a mandolin-makers
   b concert halls
   c composers

3 Why does Pelagia ask Corelli if he has heard of Greek cats?
   a She thinks it's the best way of explaining about Psipsina.
   b She wants to make him think he knows nothing.
   c Her father told her to say that to Corelli.

4 What does Corelli mean by 'Even the cats were from another planet' (line 38)?
   a They are nothing like any cats he has known before.
   b They are aliens from outer space.
   c They are the most beautiful cats he has ever seen.

93

Captain Corelli's Mandolin

D Discussion

1 Corelli thought that 'Army life consisted mainly of being paid for sitting about doing nothing' (line 4). Perhaps he should have realised there would be a war one day, and he would have to fight. What do you think? Would *you* join your country's army **a** as a profession or **b** if there was a war?

2 Why does Pelagia tell Corelli about her secret desire to be a doctor? Why hasn't she ever told her father this? Is it sometimes easier to tell your secrets to a stranger? Why is this?

3 The doctor and Pelagia are trying to make life difficult for the Italian invaders. Do you admire them for that or not? How would *you* react in their situation?

E Prediction

1 What do you think happens in the next part of the book? Choose **a**, **b** or **c**.
  a Corelli and Pelagia fall in love.
  b The doctor and Pelagia make Corelli leave their house.
  c Corelli discovers a terrible secret about the island.

2 What do you think happens at the end of the book? Choose **a**, **b** or **c**.
  a The doctor, Corelli and Pelagia die when an earthquake shakes the island.
  b Corelli returns to Italy after the war and doesn't see Pelagia again.
  c Corelli and Pelagia are apart for many years and then rediscover each other.
What would you *like* to happen in the end?

Language work

A 'There's not much demand, so you have to be very good' (line 8). *So* is a linking word. Match the parts of the sentences, and join them with the correct linking word from the box.

or	in order to	because	so that
	although	after	

1 He passed the test
2 I'll have to go to the market
3 Jane studied Thai
4 We could either eat indoors
5 Ted went by coach, not train,
6 Come round for a coffee

a she could talk to the local people in Bangkok.
b you've finished work.
c have a barbecue outside.
d he didn't do much work for it!
e we've run out of vegetables.
f save money.

Now make your own sentences using two of the linking words or phrases.

B 'What is it?' (line 24). *What* is a question-word. Complete the questions with the correct question-word from the box; there is an extra word you don't need. Then answer the questions (you will find the answers earlier in this unit).

Where	When	Who	Which	Whose
	What	How		

1 _____ wrote *Captain Corelli's Mandolin*?
2 _____ was it first published?
3 _____ in the world does the story take place?
4 _____ is a mandolin?
5 _____ bed is Corelli sleeping in?
6 _____ does the doctor feel about Corelli?

Role play

Student A: You are visiting a country for the first time, and have just met an attractive boy/girl from that country (Student B). You don't speak each other's language, so it's lucky you both speak English. Ask Student B about his or her different customs and traditions, as a way of making conversation. Actually, you are more interested in your new friend than the customs and traditions, but don't let that show.

Student B: You have realised that Student A is more interested in you than in your country's traditions, but you want to make him or her suffer a little before agreeing to meet again! So go into great detail about your festivals, ceremonies, food specialities, etc. When your new friend starts looking really bored, you feel sorry for him or her and perhaps you will arrange to meet for a coffee later.

22 Catherine Chidgey
1970–

Catherine Chidgey was born and grew up in Lower Hutt, near Wellington, on the North Island of New Zealand. She studied creative writing, psychology and German literature, and has degrees in all three. In the mid-1990s she spent two years in Berlin, Germany, on a writing scholarship. In 1998 her first novel, *In a Fishbone Church*, was published. It was a best-seller in New Zealand and was highly praised in the UK and Australia; it won three awards for a writer's best first book – the Montana New Zealand Award, the Betty Trask Award in England, and the Commonwealth Writers Prize. Since then she has received several grants and fellowships in order to continue her writing, and has published short stories in magazines and in collections. Her second novel, *Golden Deeds*, was published in 2000. In 2002 she won the Glen Schaeffer Prize in Modern Letters.

Catherine Chidgey lives in Auckland, New Zealand.

Other works by Catherine Chidgey: *In a Fishbone Church*, *The Transformation*.

Golden Deeds

Colette Hawkins has moved away from her family home to the North Island of New Zealand, in order to lead a more independent life as a student. She is surprised to receive a letter posted in England, from 'The Friends of Patrick Mercer'.

Before you read

1 What do you think a 'golden deed' is? Choose **a**, **b**, **c** or **d**.

   a a heroic, noble action which helps other people
   b a way of making a lot of money
   c a death which saves another person's life
   d a person who is skilled at working with gold

2 Why do you think Colette is surprised to receive the letter? Choose **a**, **b**, **c** or **d**.

   a She has never been to Europe.
   b She thinks no one knows her new address.
   c She can't remember meeting Patrick.
   d She thinks she has no friends at all.

Now read the first text.

Think about these questions as you read. Is the text …

… exciting?   … funny?   … difficult?   … scary?   … sad?   … interesting?

18 October 1999

Dear Colette,

As you will have heard, Patrick is still in a serious condition in Saint Luke's Hospital. While we're able to visit him every day, we're aware that many of his friends don't live locally, so to keep you all up to date on his progress, we've decided to start this newsletter.

We're happy to report that his leg and his ribs are healing, and the bruising on his chest is much improved. The grafts on his arm are taking longer, but thanks to the wonderful surgeons here there shouldn't be much scarring. At this stage, of course, Patrick is still unconscious, so one of our main objectives is to talk to him as much as possible. We're asking all of his friends to send letters which can be read out to him, or tapes. If you do happen to be in the area, naturally you're most welcome to visit him at Saint Luke's.

When he returns home, Patrick will be facing a number of costs. To help meet these, we've established a bank account in his name, and any donations would be gratefully received.

So that we can provide you with regular updates on Patrick's progress, please be sure to let us know if your contact details change. In the meantime, we hope you will help in any way you can.

With best wishes,

The Friends of Patrick Mercer

> **Notes** [Some of the words and expressions are dealt with in *Working with the text*.]
>
> *keep you all up to date* (line 5): give you the latest information
> *newsletter* (line 5): an information sheet sent out regularly
> *ribs* (line 6): the bones of your chest
> *bruising* (line 6): damaged skin, often black, blue or yellow for a while
> *grafts* (line 7): skin taken from another part of the body to cover burnt skin
> *scarring* (line 8): marks showing where the skin was once cut or burnt
> *contact details* (line 16): a person's name, address and phone number

Working with the text

A The words and phrases on the left (1–6) are from the first text. Find them, then match them to their approximate meanings (a–f).

1. in a serious condition
2. locally
3. healing
4. unconscious
5. objectives
6. donations

a. getting better
b. aims, purposes
c. very ill
d. nearby, near the hospital
e. gifts of money
f. unable to talk, move, see, etc.

B True or false? Tick (✔) any true sentences and rewrite the false ones.

1. Patrick is in Saint Luke's Hospital.
2. The doctors and nurses have started a newsletter about him.
3. Patrick's leg and ribs are getting better.
4. Patrick is talking to his visitors.
5. Friends are asked to write or record messages for him.
6. Patrick is a rich man who does not need his friends' money.
7. Patrick wants to know if Colette changes her address.

C Reading between the lines

1. Why do you think Patrick is in hospital? What probably happened to him, to cause his injuries?
2. Did Patrick need an operation? How do you know?
3. What do 'The Friends of Patrick Mercer' think about the hospital staff?
4. Why is it important to talk to a person who is unconscious? How can letters or tapes help his recovery?

D Discussion

1. Why do you think Patrick 'will be facing a number of costs' (line 12) when he gets home? What do you imagine his age/job/lifestyle is like?
2. Does it seem strange, asking his friends to send money? Or is it a sensible idea? Would *you* send money to help a friend in hospital?

Now read the second text.

Every contact leaves a trace. Colette re-read the letter and tried to remember if she knew a Patrick Mercer, whether he was someone who should be familiar to her, whether she might have met him when she was overseas. *As you will have heard*, the first line assumed. She wondered how concerned she should be about his hospitalisation, his serious condition, his bruises and grafts. His unconsciousness. There was her own name at the top of the letter, added by hand in the space after *Dear*, and her own address – her mother's address – on the envelope. *We're asking all of his friends to send letters which can be read out to him, or tapes.* Surely, she thought, she wouldn't have forgotten a friend. She ran her finger over the stamp as if doing so might provide her with a clue. She checked inside the envelope for something she might have missed, some other document which explained everything. On the back was an English address she didn't recognise. Perhaps, she thought, she'd been at school with him. Most of her year were overseas now, New Zealand having become too small for them. She studied the tiny alpine scene on the stamp. There appeared to be a figure standing on the mountain, legs astride. An English explorer, perhaps, anonymous in his fur-lined cladding, about to plant a flag into the snow. Colette held the envelope right up to her eye, so close she could smell the sour white paper, but the explorer was inked over with a blurry date. It dirtied the whole mountain, and she couldn't be sure he was there at all.

Notes
trace (line 20): a sign that someone was there
overseas (line 22): abroad, in a foreign country
her mother's address (line 26): her mother sent the letter on to her
most of her year (line 32): most of the students in her age-group at school
alpine (line 33): of the Alps, a mountain range in south central Europe
legs astride (line 34): standing with legs apart
anonymous (line 35): describes a person whose name is unknown
cladding (line 35): (here) outdoor clothes
sour (line 36): (here) bitter-smelling
blurry (line 37): not clear

Working with the text

Do you like the two texts? Why or why not?

E Answer the questions.

1 Does Colette remember who Patrick is?
2 Is she worried about his poor health?
3 Is her name typed or handwritten on the letter?
4 Why does she check the inside of the envelope?
5 Where is the English address written?
6 Does she recognise the figure on the stamp?
7 Why does she hold the envelope up to her eye?
8 What does 'it' refer to in 'it dirtied the whole mountain' (line 37)?

F Reading between the lines

1 Why does Colette re-read the letter, and examine it and the envelope so carefully?
2 Colette's name is on the letter and her mother's address is on the envelope. What does that prove?
3 What does Colette think is the most likely connection between her and Patrick?
4 Why have most of Colette's fellow-pupils left New Zealand?

G Discussion

1 Who do you think Patrick is? Choose **a**, **b**, **c** or **d**.

   a an old schoolfriend of Colette's
   b someone who once loved Colette's mother
   c someone Colette met on a foreign holiday
   d a criminal who wants money from Colette

2 What would *you* do in Colette's situation? Send a letter, a tape, some money? Do nothing? Or do something else – what?

H Prediction

What do you think happens in the end? Choose **a**, **b**, **c** or **d**.

   a Patrick dies before Colette can find out who he is.
   b Colette flies to England to visit Patrick.
   c Colette writes to Patrick and discovers he was once her boyfriend.
   d Patrick explains that he is Colette's father.

Golden Deeds

Language work

A '... his leg and his ribs are healing' (line 6). *Are healing* is an example of the present continuous, to talk about something happening now. Match these parts of present continuous sentences.

1. The President is setting off
2. House prices are going up
3. The Government is suggesting
4. The police are keeping a close eye
5. Many British people are buying cars direct

a changes to the transport system.
b from the manufacturer these days.
c all round the country.
d on a four-day visit to Jordan today.
e on travelling football fans.

B '... we've decided to start this newsletter' (line 5). *We've decided* is an example of the present perfect. *We've* is a short form of *We have*. Complete the sentences with the correct present perfect form of the verbs in brackets.

1. I think we _____ a mistake – this is the wrong house! (make)
2. So far today I _____ the grass and _____ the apples. (cut, pick)
3. You can see she's tired. She _____ just _____ all the way to Strasbourg and back! (drive)
4. Thanks for the invitation, but I _____ already _____ lunch. (have)
5. Our new secretary _____ how to set the alarm yet. (not learn)
6. My aunt _____ just _____ down the stairs – ring for the ambulance, quickly! (fall)

C 'When he returns home' (line 12). After *when, while, until, before, after* and *as soon as* with a future idea, we use the present simple, not a future form. Some of these sentences have a mistake in them. Tick (✔) any correct sentences and rewrite the wrong ones.

1. I'll wait here until the taxi will come.
2. We'll get on the train as soon as my brother arrives.
3. Read the instructions before you will start cooking.
4. I'll check our e-mails while you'll unpack the car.
5. He'll ring you back after he gets home.
6. We'll have to tidy up the house really well when the party's over.

Role play

Student A: Someone has sent you an e-mail telling you about an old schoolfriend who has had a car accident and is ill in hospital. You remember your friend very well, and are sorry you haven't been in touch recently. The e-mail asks you to visit the schoolfriend and/or send money to help pay his or her bills when he or she comes out of hospital. Discuss with another friend (Student B) what you should do.

Student B: You don't know Student A's old friend, but you think it's important to keep in touch with friends if possible. You think Student A should write or make a visit to the hospital. You don't like the idea of sending money – how can Student A be sure the money will really be used to pay the schoolfriend's bills? And of course the e-mail could be a hoax – a kind of joke – just a way of getting money out of people.

Writing

Imagine you are Colette. You have come to England for a few days. Write a postcard (35–45 words) to your mother. In your card, say:

- what the weather is like
- where you are staying
- what you are planning to do in England.

23 Harper Lee
1926–

Nelle Harper Lee was born in Monroeville, Alabama, USA. Her father was elected to the Alabama state legislature for twelve years; the character of Atticus Finch, hero of *To Kill a Mockingbird*, was based on him. She studied law at the University of Alabama, and moved to New York in 1950. Here she worked in the reservations department of an international airline for a while, but when friends offered to lend her enough money to start writing full-time, she left her job and wrote the first draft of *To Kill a Mockingbird*. It was published in 1960, during a period of extreme racial tension in the USA, and was hugely successful. She won the 1961 Pulitzer Prize for it – the first woman to win this prize since 1942. It was filmed in 1962, starring Gregory Peck as Atticus Finch.

Harper Lee never tried to follow up her first success. She lives in Monroeville, the small town on which she based Maycomb in *To Kill a Mockingbird*. Her interests are 19th-century literature, 18th-century music, watching politicians and cats, travelling and being alone.

To Kill a Mockingbird

This is one of the best-selling and best-loved books of all time. The story is set in a southern state of the United States of America, and is told by an eight-year-old girl, Jean Louise Finch, often called Scout. She describes her happy childhood in a small, dusty town called Maycomb, and her adventures with her older brother Jem. Her father, Atticus, is a lawyer, and the book's atmosphere darkens when he defends a black man, Tom Robinson, in an important court case. Tom is accused of raping a white woman. If the court finds him guilty, the punishment is death. Many people in Maycomb think Tom is guilty, just because he's black, but Atticus is brave enough to defend him and try to prove he's innocent.

It is late, on a hot summer evening, and the court case is coming to an end. Jem and Scout are sitting high up in the balcony of the court-room, which is crowded with townspeople, waiting to hear what the jury have decided. The children are hoping their father will win the case, and Tom will be found not guilty. Scout is tired from the long day in court.

Before you read

What do you think the book's title, *To Kill a Mockingbird*, means? Choose **a**, **b**, **c** or **d**.

a to kill someone who is innocent
b to kill something that is worth a lot of money
c to do something seriously wrong
d to stop someone criticising you

Now read the text up to 'no different from a winter morning.' (line 9).

Think about these questions as you read. Is the text …

… exciting?   … funny?   … difficult?   … scary?   … sad?   … interesting?

But I must have been reasonably awake, or I would not have received the impression that was creeping into me. It was not unlike one I had last winter, and I shivered, though the night was hot. The feeling grew until the atmosphere in the court-room was exactly the same as a cold February morning, when the mockingbirds were still, and the carpenters had stopped hammering on Miss Maudie's new house, and every wood door in the neighbourhood was shut as tight as the doors of the Radley Place. A deserted, waiting, empty street, and the court-room was packed with people. A steaming summer night was no different from a winter morning.

* * * * *

Mr Tate said, 'This court will come to order,' in a voice that rang with authority, and the heads below us jerked up. Mr Tate left the room and returned with Tom Robinson. He steered Tom to his place beside Atticus, and stood there. Judge Taylor had roused himself to sudden alertness and was sitting up straight, looking at the empty jury box.

What happened after that had a dreamlike quality: in a dream I saw the jury return, moving like underwater swimmers, and Judge Taylor's voice came from far away, and was tiny. I saw something only a lawyer's child could be expected to see, could be expected to watch for, and it was like watching Atticus walk into the street, raise a rifle to his shoulder and pull the trigger, but watching all the time knowing that the gun was empty.

A jury never looks at a defendant it has convicted, and when this jury came in, not one of them looked at Tom Robinson. The foreman handed a piece of paper to Mr Tate who handed it to the clerk who handed it to the judge...

I shut my eyes. Judge Taylor was polling the jury: 'Guilty... guilty... guilty... guilty...' I peeked at Jem: his hands were white from gripping the balcony rail, and his shoulders jerked as if each 'guilty' was a separate stab between them.

Judge Taylor was saying something. His gavel was in his fist, but he wasn't using it. Dimly, I saw Atticus pushing papers from the table into his brief-case. He snapped it shut, went to the court reporter and said something, nodded to Mr Gilmer, and then went to Tom Robinson and whispered something to him. Atticus put his hand on Tom's shoulder as he whispered. Atticus took his coat off the back of his chair and pulled it over his shoulder. Then he left the court-room, but not by his usual exit. He must have wanted to go home the short way, because he walked quickly down the middle aisle towards the south exit. I followed the top of his head as he made his way to the door. He did not look up.

Someone was punching me, but I was reluctant to take my eyes from the people below us, and from the image of Atticus's lonely walk down the aisle.

'Miss Jean Louise?'

I looked around. They were standing. All around us and in the balcony on the opposite wall, the Negroes were getting to their feet. Reverend Sykes's voice was as distant as Judge Taylor's:

'Miss Jean Louise, stand up. Your father's passin'.'

Harper Lee

Notes [Some of the words and expressions are dealt with in *Working with the text*.]

shivered (line 3): shook suddenly, because of cold or fear
mockingbirds (line 5): American songbirds
the Radley Place (line 7): a house where the Radley family lived
deserted (line 7): completely empty of people
steaming (line 8): very hot and damp
Mr Tate (line 10): the local police officer or sheriff
This court will come to order (line 10): said when a court case is about to begin
jury (line 14): twelve people who decide if the accused is guilty or not
trigger (line 19): you pull this on a gun to fire it
defendant (line 21): the accused person
convicted (line 21): found guilty
foreman (line 22): the leader of the jury
polling (line 24): asking for their opinions
guilty (line 24): describes someone who has committed a crime
gavel (line 27): the judge's hammer; he hits his desk with it to quieten the court
dimly (line 28): faintly, with difficulty
Mr Gilmer (line 29): the prosecuting lawyer
Negroes (line 40): (old-fashioned and now often considered offensive) black people of African origin
getting to their feet (line 40): standing up
Reverend Sykes (line 40): a black priest watching the court case

Working with the text

A The phrases on the left (1–4) are from the text. Find them, then match them with their approximate meanings (a–d).

1 that was creeping into me
2 not unlike
3 shut as tight as
4 packed with people

a I was beginning to feel
b closed as firmly as
c crowded
d almost the same as

B Discussion

1 What do you think happened on that cold February morning? Choose **a**, **b**, **c** or **d**.

  a A murderer escaped from the local prison.
  b The river was about to flood the town.
  c A mad dog came down the street.
  d something else

2 Why were the doors of the Radley Place shut so tightly then? Choose **a**, **b**, **c** or **d**.

  a Nobody lived there any more.
  b A very shy person lived there.
  c An old lady was lying ill in there.
  d something else

C Prediction

What do you think happens next? Choose **a**, **b** or **c**.

a The jury finds Tom not guilty.
b The jury finds Tom guilty.
c The jury cannot decide.

Now read to the end of the text.

Do you like the text? Why or why not?

D The words on the left (1–5) are from the second part of the text. Find them, then match them with their approximate meanings (a–e).

1 alertness
2 tiny
3 exit
4 aisle
5 reluctant

a a path between the seats
b unwilling
c being awake, noticing things
d a way out of a building
e very small and faint

E Reading between the lines

1 What does Scout notice – 'something only a lawyer's child could be expected to see' (line 17)?
2 Why do you think she compares this to seeing her father fire an empty gun?
3 How do you think Jem feels about the jury's decision?
4 How do you think Atticus feels about the jury's decision?
5 Who do you think is 'punching' Scout, and why?

To Kill a Mockingbird

F Complete the sentences about the story with the correct word from the box.

> judge   lawyers   jury   court case
> court-room   foreman   convicted   gavel

1 All the people sitting in the crowded _____ were waiting for the _____ to give its decision.
2 The _____ asked the jury what it had decided, and the _____ gave a piece of paper to the sheriff.
3 Judge Taylor was ready to hit the desk with his _____, but that wasn't necessary.
4 Mr Gilmer and Atticus Finch were the two _____ involved.
5 It was probably the most important _____ Atticus had ever worked on.
6 Unfortunately Tom Robinson was _____ by the court.

G Discussion

1 Do you agree that some crimes are so bad that death is the correct punishment? Which ones?
2 Do you admire lawyers like Atticus Finch, who take on unpopular cases because they believe it's the right thing to do? Would *you* like to be a lawyer yourself?

H Prediction

What do you think happens in the rest of the story? Choose **a**, **b**, **c** or **d**.

a Tom is put to death.
b Atticus appeals, and in the next court case Tom is proved innocent.
c Tom is shot while trying to escape.
d Tom's accusers try to kill Atticus.

Language work

A '... though the night was hot' (line 3). *Though* is a linking word, short for *although*. Match the parts of sentences, linking them with the correct word or phrase from the box.

> as soon as   and   because   in order to   but

1 Sonia's going to Peru
2 My sister learnt to drive
3 I'll meet you at the café
4 We can't stay at the hotel
5 It was a very hot day

a we haven't got any money!
b I finish work.
c nobody was swimming.
d soon bought a car.
e study the Incas.

B 'Dimly, I saw Atticus' (line 28). The usual way to make an adverb, like *dimly*, is to add *-ly* to the adjective (*dim* + *-ly* = *dimly*). Complete the sentences with the correct adverb form of the adjectives in the box.

> loud   stupid   sad   slow   quiet

1 Sit there _____ please! No talking!
2 _____, I couldn't afford a holiday last year. It really was a pity.
3 This train's going so _____! I don't think we'll get there in time.
4 _____, I forgot to give my name and address.
5 I think she talks too _____. You can hear her from the other side of the room!

Writing

This is part of a letter you receive from an English penfriend.

I live with my grandmother, my parents and my little sister in a flat in the centre of town. What about you and your family? Where do you live?

Now write a letter (about 100 words) answering your penfriend's questions.

24 DIANA SOUHAMI
1940–

Diana Souhami was born in London, England. She has written many highly-praised books. *The Trials of Radclyffe Hall* was shortlisted for the James Tait Black Prize for Biography and won the US Lambda Literary Award. *Mrs Keppel and Her Daughters* was a best-seller. *Selkirk's Island*, published in 2001, won the Whitbread Biography Award. She has also written plays for radio, television and theatre.

Diana Souhami lives in London and Devon, England.

Other works by Diana Souhami: *The Trials of Radclyffe Hall, Mrs Keppel and Her Daughters, Gertrude and Alice, Greta and Cecil, Gluck: Her Biography, Wild Girls.*

Selkirk's Island

Most people have heard of Robinson Crusoe, the sailor who saved himself from shipwreck and lived alone on a desert island for nearly thirty years. *Robinson Crusoe* was written by Daniel Defoe in 1719. He based it on a real event which had happened in 1704 – a Scottish sailor called Alexander Selkirk was left to die on a desert island, and had to learn how to survive there with no help from anyone. *Selkirk's Island* is the story of Selkirk's life.

It is 1704. The British ship *Cinque Ports* has been at sea for over a year, searching for and attacking Spanish and Portuguese ships, in order to take the gold, silver and any other valuables they are carrying. So far the sailors have received very little treasure, and the ship is now in very bad condition. The crew have landed on an island in the eastern Pacific Ocean, to take on fresh food and water. Captain Stradling insists that they must continue their journey, but Alexander Selkirk, an experienced sailor, thinks the ship is not safe to sail in.

Before you read

If you were left alone on a desert island, what would the biggest problem be? Tick (✔) one of these.

- dying of thirst or hunger
- being attacked by wild animals
- going mad through loneliness
- drowning as you try to swim away

How do you think *you* would manage if you were left on a desert island?

Now read the first text.

Think about these questions as you read. Is the text …

… exciting?   … funny?   … difficult?   … scary?   … sad?   … interesting?

At the beginning of October Stradling gave orders to sail. Selkirk advised the crew to refuse. It was his view that in this ship none of them would go anywhere but to the ocean floor.

... Stradling accused him of inciting mutiny. He told him he would have his wish and stay on The Island: it was better than he deserved.

Selkirk's concern about the ship was justified. But no one elected to stay with him. No friend. ...

Stradling ordered Selkirk's sea chest, clothes and bedding to be put ashore. Selkirk watched from the beach as the men prepared to leave. ...

He asked Stradling to forgive him, to let him rejoin the ship. He said he would comply. Stradling told him to go to hell, he could be food for vultures for all he cared. He hoped his fate would be a lesson to the other men.

Selkirk watched as the small boats prepared to leave the shore. He lumbered over the stones and tried to get on board but was pushed back. He waded into the water, pleading. He watched as the anchor was drawn and the ship towed to the open sea. ... There was a light breeze from the west. The ship slipped behind the cliff face and from his view.

 .....

All courage left him when the ship was gone. The sea stretched out. ... The sea that had beckoned freedom and fortune now locked him in.

Thomas Jones, James Ryder, William Shribes, John Cobham... He thought they would come back for him. He stayed by the shore, scanning the ocean. Whatever their fate he now wanted to be with them. If their ship sank he would choose to go down with it. It was his ship too.

Laurence Wellbroke, Martin Cooke, Christian Fletcher, Peter Haywood ... they defined his world. The voyage they had made together was for more than gold: it was to show courage, to have a common purpose, to be men. Without them The Island was a prison and he a mariner without a ship, a man without a voice.

Notes [Some of the words and expressions are dealt with in *Working with the text*.]

crew (line 1): the sailors who work on a ship
inciting mutiny (line 4): encouraging sailors to disobey their captain
justified (line 6): reasonable
elected (line 6): (here) chose
sea chest (line 8): wooden chest containing a sailor's things
ashore (line 8): on the beach, on land
comply (line 11): (here) do what Stradling wanted
vultures (line 11): large birds which eat the flesh of dead bodies
for all he cared (line 11): he did not care what happened to Selkirk
fate (line 12): what happens to a person in the end
lumbered (line 13): ran heavily
waded (line 14): walked into the water
pleading (line 15): begging, asking desperately
the anchor was drawn (line 15): the crew pulled up the heavy metal weight holding the ship in place
the ship (was) towed (line 15): men in small rowing boats pulled the ship away from land
cliff face (line 16): high, steep side of a hill overlooking the sea
stretched out (line 18): looked enormously wide
beckoned (line 19): (here) seemed to offer
fortune (line 19): riches, wealth
Thomas Jones ... John Cobham (line 20): men from the Cinque Ports' crew
scanning the ocean (line 21): looking over the whole sea
Laurence Wellbroke ... Peter Haywood (line 24): more of Selkirk's fellow sailors
they defined his world (line 24): they were a very important part of his life
voyage (line 25): sea journey
mariner (line 27): sailor

Working with the text

A The phrases on the left (1–5) are from the first text. Find them, then match them with their approximate meanings (a–e).

1. orders to sail
2. the ocean floor
3. better than he deserved
4. be food for vultures
5. be a lesson to the other men

a. the bottom of the sea
b. more than he could expect
c. die and be eaten by birds
d. show the crew they must obey orders
e. the command to go to sea

B Reading between the lines

1. What does Selkirk think will happen to the crew if the ship goes to sea?
2. Why does Selkirk's advice to the crew count as mutiny?
3. What does Stradling mean when he says Selkirk can 'have his wish' (line 4)?
4. Why does Selkirk change his mind and ask Stradling to forgive him?
5. Why does Selkirk think the crew will come back for him?
6. How does Selkirk feel about his fellow sailors?
7. What does he think a sailor without a ship is like?

C Match these parts of sentences from the first text. Try to do it from memory, then check with the text.

1. All courage left him
2. He thought
3. He stayed by the shore,
4. Whatever their fate
5. If their ship sank
6. The voyage they had made together

a. was for more than gold.
b. he now wanted to be with them.
c. scanning the ocean.
d. he would choose to go down with it.
e. when the ship was gone.
f. they would come back for him.

D Prediction

How do you think Selkirk manages on the island? Tick (✔) as many as you like.

a. He catches fish and hunts animals to eat.
b. He builds a small wooden house.
c. He keeps a fire going so that passing ships can see it.
d. He keeps a diary of his stay on the island.

Now read the second text.

The year is now 1709.

Selkirk was cooking food by his hut in the late afternoon, when the ship of rescue came. He judged the month to be late January. He scanned the sea and there, on the horizon, was a wooden ship with white sails. He knew that it was his ship. It was so much the ship of his dreams.

In the moment of seeing it time stopped. There seemed no interval between the point of abandonment and this promise of rescue. The same wide bay, the straight line of the horizon, the high cliffs and wheeling birds. Nothing had happened between then and now. ... He had been nothing to anyone. A shadow of self.

A second ship came into view. ... He felt in conflict, fearing the ships would pass, wanting them to pass, fearing ... the sullying of The Island. He supposed that the same men had come back for him, that Stradling was the captain of the smaller vessel. He hated him as acutely as the day they had quarrelled. He would rather die alone in the mountains than see him face to face.

The ships were heading east. He thought they would miss The Island, it was such a small block of land. ...

Selkirk dragged a burning log to the beach. It was meant as his beacon of welcome. He wanted to show that his was the bay of safety, that here were warmth, food and water.

Notes
hut (line 28): small wooden house
ship of rescue (line 28): a ship that would save him
abandonment (line 33): being left on the island to die
bay (line 33): the curve of the coastline, a sheltered place for boats to land
horizon (line 34): the line where the sea seems to meet the sky
wheeling (line 34): flying around in circles
in conflict (line 36): confused, wanting two opposite things
sullying (line 37): dirtying, spoiling
vessel (line 39): ship
acutely (line 39): sharply, strongly
log (line 43): a piece of dead wood
beacon (line 43): fire used to signal to ships

Working with the text

Do you like the two texts? Why or why not?

E Answer the questions.

1 How long has Selkirk been on the island now?
2 What can he see on the horizon?
3 Why does he feel 'in conflict' (line 36)?
4 How does he feel about Stradling?
5 Why is it easy for ships to miss the island?
6 Why does Selkirk drag a burning log to the beach?

F Reading between the lines

1 How do we know that Selkirk has often hoped for a 'ship of rescue' (line 28)?
2 Why does Selkirk have the feeling that 'time stopped' (line 32)?
3 How does Selkirk feel about the island – 'fearing... the sullying of The Island' (line 37) – and why?
4 Do you think Selkirk will refuse to be rescued if Stradling is on one of the ships?

G Discussion

1 Why was mutiny considered such a serious crime in the 17th and 18th centuries? What do you think the usual punishment for it was? Was Stradling right to leave Selkirk alone on the island to die?
2 Why do you think Stradling and Selkirk hate each other so much?
3 What would *you* do if you were left alone on a desert island?

H Prediction

1 What do you think happens next? Choose **a**, **b**, **c** or **d**.

   a Selkirk is rescued and makes a fortune out of telling his story.
   b The ships do not see the island, and sail past.
   c Stradling is on board one of the ships, so Selkirk stays on the island.
   d Selkirk is rescued and goes on several more voyages.

2 What do you think happens to Selkirk in the end? Choose **a**, **b** or **c**.

   a He dies alone on the island.
   b He dies of an illness on a future voyage.
   c He dies at home in Scotland in the arms of his wife.

Selkirk's Island

Language work

A '(Selkirk) was pushed back' (line 14). *Was pushed* is an example of the past simple passive. Complete the sentences about the first text with the correct past simple passive form of the verbs in brackets.

1 Selkirk _____ by Stradling. (not forgive)
2 Selkirk _____ he would have to stay on the island. (tell)
3 His sea chest _____, and the crew put it ashore. (pack)
4 He _____ alone on the shore, as the boats moved away. (leave)
5 The anchor _____, and the ship _____ out to the open sea. (pull up, tow)

B 'He thought they would come back for him' (line 20). This is an example of reported speech. Put these sentences into reported speech, starting with *She said* each time.

1 'The bus could be about fifteen minutes late.'
2 'They'll pay for everything.'
3 'I'll let you know as soon as possible.'
4 'I've been there before.'
5 'They don't understand the problem.'
6 'There's no cheese left in the fridge.'

C 'A second ship came into view' (line 36). The indefinite article is *a/an*. The definite article is *the*. Complete the sentences with *a, an, the* or –.

1 He's _____ well-known judge.
2 She's _____ excellent teacher.
3 Brussels is _____ European city.
4 I had to go to _____ town hall.
5 She sailed solo across _____ Pacific.
6 They get paid £100 _____ hour!
7 He often visits _____ USA.
8 I think _____ fruit is good for you.
9 Have _____ cup of coffee?
10 Well, _____ life's fun, isn't it?

Role play

Student A: You and your friend (Student B) have just watched a TV documentary about a glamorous film star who was left on a desert island for a few days. According to the programme, this film star managed to find her own food and fresh water, and build a hut and a boat. She enjoyed herself so much that she did not want to leave when the 'rescue ship' came for her a week later! You don't believe she did all this without any help, and you are disgusted with the film star for pretending. Discuss your opinions with Student B.

Student B: You disagree with Student A. You think anybody with a little intelligence could survive on a desert island for a week, and you admire the film star for doing it. Explain what you think she did every day, and how differently *you* would do things if *you* were on a desert island.

Writing

Imagine you are Alexander Selkirk, alone on the island. Write a message (35–45 words) on a piece of paper. Your plan is to put the message inside a bottle and throw the bottle into the sea, hoping that the crew of a passing ship will find it and rescue you. In your message:

- say who you are
- explain where you are
- ask for help.

25 BEN OKRI
1959–

Ben Okri was born in Minna, Nigeria. He was educated in Nigeria, and at the University of Essex in England, where he studied Comparative Literature. He was poetry editor for *West Africa* magazine (1983–1986) and broadcast regularly for the BBC World Service (1983–1985). He was appointed Fellow Commoner in Creative Arts at Trinity College Cambridge, a post he held until 1993, and he became a Fellow of the Royal Society of Literature in 1987. His first two novels, *Flowers and Shadows* (1980) and *The Landscapes Within* (1981), are both set in Nigeria; in both of these, the author explores the political violence and human suffering that he himself saw during the civil war in Nigeria. Ben Okri has won many awards for his writing, but perhaps his greatest achievement was winning the 1991 Booker Prize for his novel *The Famished Road*, which was published in that year.

Ben Okri was awarded an OBE (Officer of the Order of the British Empire) in 2001. He lives in London, England.

Other works by Ben Okri: (novels) *Flowers and Shadows, The Landscapes Within, Songs of Enchantment, Astonishing the Gods, Dangerous Love, Infinite Riches, In Arcadia*; (short stories) *Incidents at the Shrine, Stars of the New Curfew*; (poetry) *An African Elegy, Mental Flight*.

The Famished Road

Azaro is a spirit-child who is telling the story, which takes place in an African country. Because he loves his human mother, Azaro has chosen not to return to the spirit world but to stay in the world of the living. He is an observer of his family and his countrymen, and he describes in detail the joys and sorrows of their daily lives.

Before you read

Famished means extremely hungry, so what do you think the title, *The Famished Road*, means? Tick (✔) as many as you like.

a   a road of houses, where everybody is hungry
b   a way for a nation to improve people's lives, so that they are never hungry again
c   a spirit which takes the shape of a road, and swallows people up
d   a plan for developing a country, which destroys as much as it builds

Now read to the end of the text.

Think about these questions as you read. Is the text …

… exciting?   … funny?   … difficult?   … scary?   … sad?   … interesting?

Sunday brought us the secret faces of politics.

Dad's relations came to visit. They came with their children, all of them stiff and shy in the good clothes they rarely wore. We didn't have enough chairs for them and Mum had to swallow her pride and borrow chairs from our neighbours. The compound was aflame with politics. Our relations came to visit, but they also came to criticise. They attacked Dad for not visiting them, for not attending the meetings of our townspeople, for not contributing to wedding presents, funeral arrangements, and endless financial engagements. Dad responded badly to their criticisms. He blamed them for not helping him, for not being visible during his times of crisis; and their recriminations flew back and forth, developed into terrible arguments, with everyone shouting at the top of their voices, till they all seemed more like implacable enemies than like members of an extended family.

They seemed so much against one another that I felt ashamed being in the room, witnessing it all. The wives and children of our relations avoided looking at me and then I suspected that they hated us as much as we avoided their company. After a long period of shouting one of our relations tried to change the subject by bringing up politics and the coming elections. It was the most unfortunate change of subject. Another great altercation started and burned vehemently in the small room. Dad, who supported the Party for the Poor, quivered during the argument, unable to contain his rage; our relation, who supported the Party of the Rich, was very calm, almost disdainful. He had more money than Dad and lived in a part of the city that already had electricity.

The room vibrated with their differences and at times it seemed they would fall on one another and fight out the battle of ascendancies. But Mum came in with a tray of food and drinks. Dad sent for some ogogoro and kola-nuts and made a libation, praying for harmony in the extended arms of the family. Our relations ate in silence. After they had eaten, they drank in silence. Conversation had been exhausted. When the silence got too oppressive the wives of our relations went out into the passage with Mum and I heard them laughing while the men sat in the room, embarrassed by their differences.

The afternoon intensified with the heat. Voices in the compound grew louder; children played in the passage; neighbours quarrelled; our relations said they were going; Dad didn't disguise his relief. One of the wives gave me a penny and called me a bad boy for not visiting them. Dad saw his relations off. He was away a long time. When he got back he was in quite a storm of bad temper. He raged against all relations, against all the relatives who had more money than him. He cursed their selfishness, and swore that they only came to visit to make themselves feel better in comparison with our condition. He worked himself into a tremendous verbal campaign against the Party of the Rich and in the height of his denunciation his eyes fell on the basin of powdered milk. He snatched it from the top of the cupboard and stormed out. I heard Mum pleading with him not to throw the milk away and then I heard her sigh. Dad came back with an empty basin and a wicked gleam in his eyes.

BEN OKRI

> **Notes**
> *compound* (line 5): local area of houses
> *aflame with politics* (line 5): (here) full of talk of politics
> *recriminations* (line 11): criticisms of each other
> *implacable* (line 11): impossible to make peace with
> *altercation* (line 18): argument, quarrel or disagreement
> *vehemently* (line 18): violently
> *quivered* (line 19): trembled, shook
> *rage* (line 20): anger
> *disdainful* (line 21): scornful
> *vibrated* (line 23): shook, trembled
> *the battle of ascendancies* (line 24): the fight to see who would win
>
> *ogogoro* (line 25): alcoholic drink, made from the sap (plant liquid) of palm trees
> *kola-nuts* (line 25): type of nut
> *libation* (line 25): a drink in honour of a god
> *penny* (line 33): a small coin, a little money
> *saw his relations off* (line 34): went to the door to say goodbye to his relations
> *denunciation* (line 39): criticism, accusation
> *basin* (line 40): bowl
> *powdered milk* (line 40): dried milk given to people who lived in the compound by the Party of the Rich, in order to win votes

Working with the text

Do you like the text? Why or why not?

A Answer the questions.

1 Why are Azaro's father's relations 'stiff and shy' (line 2)?
2 Why do they criticise Azaro's father?
3 How does he reply to their accusations?
4 Which are the two main political parties in this country?
5 Why does one of the relations support the Party of the Rich?
6 How does Azaro's mother prevent a fight?

B True or false? Tick (✔) any true sentences and rewrite the false ones.

1 The relatives bring their own chairs to the house.
2 The arguments are loud and angry.
3 Azaro's parents' house has electricity.
4 Azaro's father is sorry to say goodbye to his relations.
5 Azaro's father throws away a basin of powdered milk.

C Match the adjectives (1–8) to the nouns (a–h), to make pairs of words from the text. Try to do it from memory, then check with the text.

1	secret	a	gleam
2	wedding	b	temper
3	terrible	c	faces
4	implacable	d	presents
5	great	e	arguments
6	bad	f	enemies
7	verbal	g	altercation
8	wicked	h	campaign

D Reading between the lines

1 Has Azaro's father had some difficult times in the past? How do you know?
2 Is it sensible for one of the relations to start talking about politics? Why or why not?
3 Are the wives as angry with Azaro's father as the men are? How do you know?
4 Why do you think 'voices in the compound grew louder' (line 31) during the afternoon?
5 What is the main reason why Azaro's father is angry with his relations?
6 Why do you think he throws away the powdered milk?

E Discussion

1 'Our relations came to visit, but they also came to criticise' (line 5). Do you think it's always important for people to say what they think, very honestly, or do you think they should be polite if they are visiting someone's house?
2 Is it a good idea to have arguments about politics? Do you enjoy having a lively discussion about political parties and the actions politicians should take?
3 Do people often feel angry or envious if they don't earn as much as a brother or a cousin does? Do you know how much the people in your family earn, and does it worry you or impress you?

The Famished Road

F Prediction

What do you think happens next? Tick (✔) as many as you like.

a Azaro's father makes his peace with his relations.

b Azaro's parents go out for the evening, because they are happy the relations have left.

c Azaro's father decides to earn more money in future.

d Azaro's father's relations return to say how sorry they are.

e Azaro's father decides that, after all, he agrees with his relations' political opinions.

Language work

A 'He blamed them for not helping him' (line 8). The verb *blame* takes the preposition *for*. Other verbs take other prepositions. Match the parts of sentences, and link them with the correct preposition from the box. Use each preposition only once.

| for   of   with   of   to   in   on |

1 I insist
2 We succeeded
3 The old lady accused him
4 I really object
5 Why don't you apply
6 I'm sorry, but I don't agree
7 Liz's parents didn't approve

a any of your ideas.
b Lucy's job, when she leaves?
c the man she wanted to marry.
d seeing the manager at once!
e breaking into her flat.
f people smoking during meals.
g getting the car to start.

B 'After they had eaten, they drank in silence' (line 27). The past perfect *had eaten* is used to show something happened before a past simple action, *drank*. Complete the sentences using the verbs in brackets. Use one past perfect and one past simple form in each sentence.

1 After I (have) a bath, I (go) to bed.
2 After he (do) the shopping, he (have) a coffee.
3 I (never visit) the area before we (come) to live here in 1999.
4 She (not go) with Sam to the theatre because she (already see) the play.
5 By the time she (leave) school, Susie (learn) five languages.
6 The police (tell) us they (already search) most of the forest.

Now think up your own past perfect sentence about yourself.

C 'Dad saw his relations off' (line 34). *See off* is a phrasal verb meaning *say goodbye to*, *show to the door*, *take to the station*, etc. Match the parts of sentences or conversations with phrasal verbs in them.

1 So we set off
2 Did you turn off
3 Don't tell me the car's
4 It's about time
5 Don't go without me!
6 She's getting on
7 Come and see me tomorrow, and we'll

a Hold on!
b sort out your problem then.
c on our long journey.
d the lights before you left?
e broken down again!
f you got up! It's lunchtime!
g with her project.

Role play

Student A: You are the eldest son/daughter in your family. You are still living at home, although you're grown up and have a job. You prefer to lead your own life and see your own friends, not your family. So you are shocked when your father tells you he's inviting all your relations to a big family party next weekend, and he expects you to be there. Try to put him off the whole idea, by reminding him of the terrible arguments at the last family party. If that doesn't work, tell him firmly you do not want to be involved.

Student B: You are Student A's father. You only agreed to the idea of the family party to keep your wife happy. Secretly you think it could be a disaster, but it's arranged now, so you will have to go ahead with it. You are certainly not going to let your eldest son/daughter miss it and you think he or she is just being selfish. Your younger children will be there, too, of course, and family unity is very important to you.

26 ANITA DESAI
1937–

Anita Desai was born in Mussoorie, India. Her father was Bengali and her mother was German. She was educated in Delhi. She started writing when she was six, and has written novels, short stories and children's books, mostly based on her experience of life in India. Her writing has won many prizes and awards. In 1978 her novel *Fire on the Mountain* won the Winifred Holtby Memorial Prize and the National Academy of Letters Award. In the same year *Games at Twilight and Other Stories* was published. *Clear Light of Day*, *In Custody* and *Fasting Feasting* were all shortlisted for the Booker McConnell Prize. There is a film of *In Custody*, made by Merchant Ivory Productions. She won the 1983 Guardian Children's Fiction Award for her children's book *The Village By The Sea*. She is a Fellow of the Royal Society of Literature.

Anita Desai lives in the United States, and is Professor of Writing at Massachusetts Institute of Technology.

Other works by Anita Desai: (novels) *Cry The Peacock, Voices in the City, Where Shall We Go This Summer?, Fire on the Mountain, The Peacock Garden, Clear Light of Day, In Custody, Baumgarten's Bombay, Journey to Ithaca, Fasting Feasting*; (short stories) *Diamond Dust and Other Stories*; (children's book) *The Village By The Sea*.

Studies in the Park

This short story comes from the collection *Games at Twilight and Other Stories*. It is set in a large Indian city. The person who is telling the story is a young man called Suno, who is trying to study for an important examination.

Before you read

What do you think Suno will find most difficult about studying for the exam? Tick (✔) as many as you like.

a dealing with the stress
b finding a quiet place to study
c finding a friend to study with
d making himself start studying
e understanding the notes he wrote during lessons
f finding time to phone or see his friends while he is studying

Now read to the end of the text.

Think about these questions as you read. Is the text ...

... exciting?   ... funny?   ... difficult?   ... scary?   ... sad?   ... interesting?

Studies in the Park

– Turn it off, turn it off, turn it off! First he listens to the news in Hindi. Directly after, in English. Broom – brroom – brrroom – the voice of doom roars. Next, in Tamil. Then in Punjabi. In Gujarati. What next, my god, what next? Turn it off before I smash it onto his head, fling it out of the window, do nothing of the sort of course, nothing of the sort.

– And my mother. She cuts and fries, cuts and fries. All day I hear her chopping and slicing and the pan of oil hissing. What all does she find to fry and feed us on, for God's sake? Eggplants, potatoes, spinach, shoe soles, newspapers, finally she'll slice me and feed me to my brothers and sisters. Ah, now she's turned on the tap. It's roaring and pouring, pouring and roaring into a bucket without a bottom.

– The bell rings. Voices clash, clatter and break. The tin-and-bottle man? The neighbours? The police? The Help-the-Blind man? Thieves and burglars? All of them, all of them, ten or twenty or a hundred of them, marching up the stairs, hammering at the door, breaking in and climbing over me – ten, twenty or a hundred of them.

– Then, worst of all, the milk arrives. In the tallest glass in the house. 'Suno, drink your milk. Good for you, Suno. You need it. Now, before the exams. Must have it, Suno. Drink.' The voice wheedles its way into my ear like a worm. I shudder. The table tips over. The milk runs. The tumbler clangs on the floor. 'Suno, Suno, how will you do your exams?'

– That is precisely what I ask myself. All very well to give me a room – Uncle's been pushed off on a pilgrimage to Hardwar to clear a room for me – and to bring me milk and say, 'Study, Suno, study for your exam.' What about the uproar around me? These people don't know the meaning of the word Quiet. When my mother fills buckets, sloshes the kitchen floor, fries and sizzles things in the pan, she thinks she is being Quiet. The children have never even heard the word, it amazes and puzzles them. On their way back from school they fling their satchels in at my door, then tear in to snatch them back before I tear them to bits. Bawl when I pull their ears, screech when mother whacks them. Stuff themselves with her fries and then smear the grease on my books.

Notes [Some of the words and expressions are dealt with in *Working with the text*.]

Hindi (line 1): one of the official languages of India
broom–brroom–brrroom (line 2): loud sound getting louder
doom (line 2): terrible event, disaster
Tamil (line 2): a language spoken in south India and Sri Lanka
Punjabi (line 3): a language spoken in Punjab, in north-west India
Gujarati (line 3): a language spoken in Gujarat, in western India
hissing (line 7): the noise made by hot oil in a pan
eggplants (line 8): large purple vegetables, called *aubergines* in British English
soles (line 8): the undersides of shoes, often made of leather
roaring (line 10): making a loud noise
bucket (line 10): metal container for carrying water or milk
clash / clatter / clang (lines 11 and 18): make a loud noise
wheedles its way (line 17): cleverly finds its way
shudder (line 17): shake suddenly and violently
tumbler (line 18): a glass or cup
sloshes (line 24): noisily pours water over something
sizzles (line 24): cooks noisily in hot oil
satchels (line 26): bags for carrying school books
tear in (line 26): run in
bawl (line 27): cry loudly
screech (line 27): scream
whacks (line 28): hits (them) hard
stuff themselves (line 28): eat a lot of something
smear (line 28): wipe

Working with the text

Do you like the text? Why or why not?

A Reading between the lines

1 What do you think 'it' in line 1 refers to?
2 Who do you think 'he' in line 1 is?
3 What is so depressing or terrible that it sounds like a 'voice of doom' (line 2)?
4 How does Suno feel when he says, 'Turn it off before I smash it onto his head' (line 3)?
5 What does Suno mean when he says, 'do nothing of the sort of course' (line 4)? Why do you think he will do nothing?
6 Do you think Suno's mother really slices and fries shoe soles and newspapers (line 8)? Is Suno really afraid she will slice him and feed him to the rest of the family? If not, why does he say it?
7 Who do you think says, 'Suno, drink your milk' (line 15)?
8 Whose room is Suno studying in?

B True or false? Tick (✔) any true sentences and rewrite the false ones.

1 Suno's mother spends all day and night cooking.
2 She uses plenty of bottled water in the kitchen.
3 A lot of visitors come to the house.
4 Suno throws a glass of milk on the floor.
5 Suno's parents want their son to study hard.
6 The children try to be quiet when they come home from school.

C The words on the left (1–9) are from the fifth paragraph of the text. Find them, then match them with their approximate meanings (a–i).

1	precisely	a	empty
2	pilgrimage	b	take (something) quickly
3	clear	c	loud noise and confusion
4	uproar	d	exactly
5	amazes	e	throw
6	puzzles	f	a religious journey
7	fling	g	astonishes or surprises
8	snatch	h	oil or fat
9	grease	i	worries or confuses

D The verbs on the left (1–6) are from the text. Match them with the correct preposition and noun (a–f), to make phrases from the text. Try to do it from memory first, then check with the text.

1	listens	a	at the door
2	pouring	b	over me
3	marching	c	to the news
4	hammering	d	into a bucket
5	climbing	e	for your exam
6	study	f	up the stairs

E Look back at the whole text and make a list of all the words which have something to do with noise. Most of them are verbs which sound like the noise they are describing. For example, *roaring* (a lion roars, a motorbike roars, a waterfall can roar).

Studies in the Park

F Discussion

1 What is Suno's main problem with studying? Is this the only thing that prevents him from studying, or are there other reasons? How do *you* start studying for an important exam?

2 Why do Suno's family want him to drink milk? Is there any particular food or drink that you think is good for you when you're studying?

3 Are Suno's parents helping him, or are they making the problem worse? If so, how?

4 Suno doesn't want to show his anger to his father. Why is this? Do you think all children should always be polite and respectful to their parents, no matter what the parents do?

5 What could Suno do to solve his problem? Make some suggestions.

G Prediction

What do you think happens next? Tick (✔) as many as you like. Suno …

a persuades his family to make less noise.
b finds a quieter place to study.
c gets an excellent mark in his exam.
d finds studying too stressful, and refuses to take the exam.

Language work

A 'In the tallest glass in the house' (line 15). *The tallest* is the superlative of the adjective *tall*. We add *the -est* to most short adjectives, but with longer ones we use *the most –*. *Bad* has an irregular superlative, *the worst*. Complete the sentences about the text with the correct superlative form of the adjective in brackets.

1 Suno probably thinks he lives in the _____ house in the world! (noisy)

2 Perhaps Suno's parents think he's the _____ boy they know. (lazy)

3 Suno is probably the _____ person in the house. (annoyed)

4 Suno says the _____ thing of all is when the milk arrives. (bad)

5 Suno wants to study in the _____ place he can find. (quiet)

Make three of your own superlative sentences, describing a film you've seen, a place you've visited, or an experience you've had.

B Suno didn't really think a hundred people were ringing the doorbell – he was exaggerating. We often exaggerate what we say, to show how strong our feelings are. For example, *I'm starving!* doesn't mean *I'm going to die of hunger*. It just means *I'm very hungry*. Look at the following exaggerations, and complete the second sentence to show what they really mean.

1 It's boiling outside!   It's very _____.
2 I'm exhausted!   I'm very _____.
3 It's simply freezing!   It's very _____.
4 It's a matter of life and death!   It's very _____.
5 He's a man in a million!   He's a very _____.

C 'These people don't know the meaning of the word Quiet' (line 22). What does the word 'quiet' mean to you? What does it make you think of? For example:

- a library with students reading silently
- listening to the waves of the sea
- the silence in an empty house at night

Write down your own ideas.
What kind of noise do you really like, and why?
What kind of noise do you really hate, and why?

Writing

You are studying for an important exam, but your house is too noisy. Write an e-mail (35–45 words) to an English friend of yours. In your e-mail:

- explain what your problem is
- ask if you can go and study at his or her house
- suggest a time when you could go round there and start studying.

27 JOHN STEINBECK
1902–1968

John Ernst Steinbeck was born in Salinas, California, USA. After studying science at Stanford University, he worked in a succession of jobs, as labourer, pharmacist, caretaker, fruit-picker and surveyor. His first novel, *The Cup of Gold*, was published in 1929, but it was his fourth book, *Tortilla Flat* (1935), which first attracted attention. *The Grapes of Wrath* (1939), his most popular book, tells the story of a family moving to California to look for work; it was awarded the 1940 Pulitzer Prize, and was made into a film. *The Pearl* was published in 1948. Steinbeck wrote many other novels and several collections of short stories. In 1962 he was awarded the Nobel Prize for Literature.

Other works by John Steinbeck: (short stories) *The Pastures of Heaven, The Long Valley*; (novels) *The Cup of Gold, To a God Unknown, Tortilla Flat, Of Mice and Men, The Grapes of Wrath, The Moon is Down, Cannery Row, The Wayward Bus, East of Eden, Sweet Thursday*; (non-fiction) *Once There Was a War*.

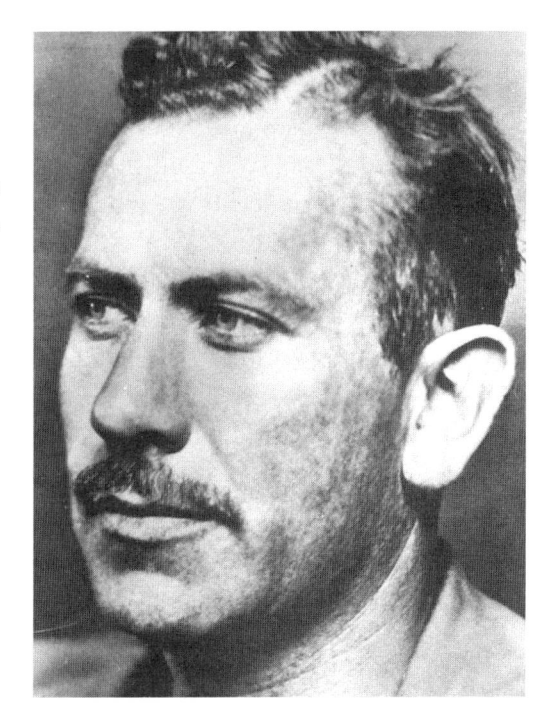

The Pearl

This is a short novel, set in a Latin American country. A young pearl fisherman, Kino, and his wife, Juana, live with their baby, Coyotito, in a small town on the coast. They are very poor, but happy. When Kino finds an enormous pearl, he imagines how rich he will be, and plans to buy new clothes for his family and even send Coyotito to school. But everyone in the town hears about the valuable pearl, and Kino kills a man who tries to steal it from him at night. Now Kino has to leave town quickly, to escape punishment for killing a man, and try to sell his pearl in one of the larger cities in the north. So he, Juana and the baby set off on a long journey, while it is still dark.

Before you read

1 What do you think is the greatest danger for Kino's family on their journey? Choose **a**, **b**, **c**, **d**, **e**, or **f**.

  a losing their way   **c** dying of hunger   **e** being attacked by thieves
  b dropping the pearl **d** being killed by wild animals **f** being arrested by the police

2 Where do you think Kino keeps the pearl hidden as they walk? Choose **a**, **b**, **c**, or **d**, and say why you have chosen it.

  a under his hat   **b** in Juana's dress   **c** in his shirt pocket   **d** in the baby's clothes

3 Where would *you* hide something valuable, if you were in a dangerous situation?

  • in one of your boots   • in a money-belt under your shirt   • in a trouser pocket
  • on a string round your neck   • in a backpack   • somewhere else – where?

Now read to the end of the text.

Think about these questions as you read. Is the text ...

... exciting?   ... funny?   ... difficult?   ... scary?   ... sad?   ... interesting?

The Pearl

The wind blew fierce and strong, and it pelted them with bits of sticks, sand, and little rocks. Juana and Kino gathered their clothing tighter about them and covered their noses and went out into the world. The sky was brushed clean by the wind and the stars were cold in a black sky. The two walked carefully, and they avoided the center of the town where some sleeper in a doorway might see them pass. For the town closed itself in against the night, and anyone who moved about in the darkness would be noticeable. Kino threaded his way around the edge of the city and turned north, north by the stars, and found the rutted sandy road that led through the brushy country towards Loreto ....

Kino could feel the blown sand against his ankles and he was glad, for he knew there would be no tracks. The little light from the stars made out for him the narrow road through the brushy country. And Kino could hear the pad of Juana's feet behind him. He went quickly and quietly, and Juana trotted behind him to keep up.

Some ancient thing stirred in Kino. Through his fear of dark and the devils that haunt the night, there came a rush of exhilaration; some animal thing was moving in him so that he was cautious and wary and dangerous; some ancient thing out of the past of his people was alive in him. The wind was at his back and the stars guided him. The wind cried and whisked in the brush, and the family went on monotonously, hour after hour. They passed no one and saw no one. At last, to their right, the waning moon arose, and when it came up the wind died down, and the land was still.

Now they could see the little road ahead of them, deep cut with sand-drifted wheel tracks. With the wind gone there would be footprints, but they were a good distance from the town and perhaps their tracks might not be noticed. Kino walked carefully in a wheel rut, and Juana followed in his path. One big cart, going to the town in the morning, could wipe out every trace of their passage.

.....

The music of the pearl was triumphant in Kino's head, and the quiet melody of the family underlay it, and they wove themselves into the soft padding of sandaled feet in the dust. All night they walked, and in the first dawn Kino searched the roadside for a covert to lie in during the day. He found his place near to the road, a little clearing where deer might have lain, and it was curtained thickly with the dry brittle trees that lined the road. And when Juana had seated herself and had settled to nurse the baby, Kino went back to the road. He broke a branch and carefully swept the footprints where they had turned from the roadway. And then, in the first light, he heard the creak of a wagon, and he crouched beside the road and watched a heavy two-wheeled cart go by ... . And when it had passed out of sight, he went back to the roadway and looked at the rut and found that the footprints were gone. And again he swept out his traces and went back to Juana.

JOHN STEINBECK

Notes [Some of the words and expressions are dealt with in *Working with the text*.]

pelted (line 1): hit
center (line 5): (American spelling) centre
for (line 5): because
threaded his way (line 7): found his way with difficulty
rutted ... road (line 8): bumpy road, not flat
brushy (line 9): with lots of low trees and bushes
Loreto (line 9): a town
tracks (line 11): signs or marks made by the family's feet
pad (line 12): soft sound of feet on the ground
trotted (line 13): walked quickly
ancient (line 14): very old
stirred (line 14): (here) moved, awoke

haunt the night (line 15): appear, are seen at night
exhilaration (line 15): excitement, joy
wary (line 16): careful, watching out for danger
whisked (line 18): (here) made a whistling noise
waning moon (line 20): the moon becoming smaller every night
wheel rut (line 25): part of the road lower than the rest, because wheels have pressed the earth down there
sandaled feet (line 28): feet wearing sandals or open shoes
covert (line 30): group of bushes and small trees where animals can hide from hunters
deer (line 31): shy wild animals with horns on their heads
brittle (line 31): easily broken
wagon (line 35): cart carrying people and their goods
crouched (line 35): bent down, hiding

Working with the text

Do you like the text? Why or why not?

A Answer the questions.

1 Kino and Juana 'covered their noses' (line 2). Why?
2 What direction is Loreto in?
3 Why is Kino pleased that it is windy?
4 At night, how can Kino see the road 'through the brushy country' (line 8)?
5 Why do Kino and Juana walk in the wheel ruts?
6 How do the family's footprints disappear from the road (three ways)?

B The words and phrases on the left (1–7) are from the text. Find them, then match them with their approximate meanings (a–g).

1	rush of exhilaration	**a**	a primitive instinct or feeling
2	some ancient thing out of the past of his people	**b**	feed the child
3	monotonously	**c**	destroy
4	wipe out	**d**	sudden joy
5	every trace of their passage	**e**	at sunrise
6	nurse the baby	**f**	doing the same thing again and again
7	in the first light	**g**	all their footprints

C True or false? Tick (✔) any true sentences, and rewrite the false ones.

1 Kino's neighbours throw sticks, sand and small rocks at him and his family.
2 A sleeper in a doorway sees the family pass by.
3 Juana walks in front of Kino.
4 Kino is afraid of being caught in a storm.
5 Kino is careful to destroy his family's tracks.

D Reading between the lines

1 What does the sky look like when it is 'brushed clean by the wind' (line 3)?
2 Why do you think Kino and Juana avoid the town centre?
3 What do you think 'the music of the pearl' (line 27) and 'the quiet melody of the family' (line 27) mean for Kino? How will they influence him?

E Discussion

1 What would *you* do in Kino's situation? How would you protect your family *and* keep the pearl?
2 Do you think Kino is too greedy? Perhaps he should be happy with Juana and the baby, and not wish for anything better. Or do you think this is Kino's chance to improve life for his family, and he deserves this good luck?

F Prediction

What do you think happens next? Choose **a**, **b** or **c**.

1 Kino ...

  a sells his pearl for a lot of money.
  b decides to throw the pearl away.
  c kills his brother for the pearl.

The Pearl

2 Juana ...
  a leaves Kino to find another husband.
  b never stops loving Kino.
  c is unhappy as a rich man's wife.

3 The baby ...
  a is killed by Kino's enemies.
  b grows up and goes to school.
  c becomes a pearl fisherman himself.

Language work

A '... the family went on monotonously, hour after hour' (line 18). *Hour after hour* is an expression using the preposition *after*. Complete these expressions with the correct preposition from the box. Use each preposition only once. There is one extra preposition that you do not need.

with	over	to	in	from	by	to

1 The two children walked hand _____ hand along the beach.
2 'Well, John, let's talk about the problem man _____ man,' my father said.
3 Day _____ day Mr Fletcher got stronger after his operation.
4 Mike and Jill are head _____ heels in love with each other, you know.
5 My brother works _____ morning _____ night. No wonder he's tired!

B 'And Kino could hear the pad of Juana's feet behind him' (line 12). The *'s* in *Juana's* shows that the feet belong to Juana. *'* is called an apostrophe. We use *'s* for a singular noun, and we usually use *s'* for a plural noun. Correct the punctuation in the following sentences.

1 The girls homework is on the table – they've just finished it.
2 Teds son is staying at Bobs house tonight.
3 The fans shouted and waved excitedly as the Real Madrid teams bus arrived.
4 I watched the postmans van drive up the hill and stop at Miss Smiths cottage.
5 Dads keys were in his pocket, but Amandas were missing.
6 Have you looked down the street? The Turners house is for sale!
7 The teachers room is on the first floor – they're having a meeting there at the moment.

C '... they avoided the center of the town where some sleeper in a doorway might see them pass' (line 4). *Where* is a relative pronoun linking the two parts of the sentence. Match these parts of sentences, and link them with the correct relative pronoun from the box. There is one extra which you do not need.

why	where	who	which	when	what

1 That's the man   a I understood the
2 Can you tell me the   truth.
  reason   b I grew up.
3 That was the moment   c owns the shop.
4 We stayed in a hotel   d was very expensive.
5 This is the town   e that happened?

Now make two sentences of your own using a relative pronoun. You could describe a person, an object, a place or an experience.

Role play

Student A: You and your friend (Student B) are living in a large city where there are a lot of poor people and the crime rate is very high. You both have to collect your pay for several months' work from the bank in cash, and then take it to your flat on the other side of town. Because it's a large amount of money, you are worried about pickpockets (street thieves). So you think you and your friend should both hide it carefully in your clothing. That way, pickpockets will not be able to grab the money as you walk through the streets.

Student B: You think your friend worries too much. No one's ever stolen anything from you, and you'd just like to see them try! What's wrong with putting all the money in a shoulder bag or a trouser pocket? You want to keep the money handy, in case you feel like spending some on the way back to your flat. Tell you friend to relax and enjoy life a bit more!

28 KAZUO ISHIGURO
1954–

Kazuo Ishiguro was born in Nagasaki, Japan. In 1960 he and his family moved to Britain, where he studied at the University of Kent and then the University of East Anglia. His writing was first noticed by the critics when he contributed three short stories to a collection of new writers' works in 1981. His first novel, *A Pale View of Hills*, was awarded the Winifred Holtby Memorial Prize by the Royal Society of Literature; it has been translated into thirteen languages. His second novel, *An Artist of the Floating World*, was shortlisted for the Booker Prize and won the Whitbread Book of the Year Award for 1986; it has been translated into fourteen languages. His best-known novel is *The Remains of the Day* (1989), which won the 1989 Booker Prize, and which was made into a film in 1993 starring Anthony Hopkins and Emma Thompson. He writes very movingly about ordinary people's feelings, especially their hopes and regrets. Despite his Japanese origin, all his books are written in English. He is a Fellow of the Royal Society of Literature and was awarded an OBE (Officer of the Order of the British Empire) in 1995.

Kazuo Ishiguro lives in London, England.

Other works by Kazuo Ishiguro: *A Pale View of Hills, An Artist of the Floating World, The Unconsoled, When We Were Orphans*.

The Remains of the Day

The story is told from the point of view of Stevens, an elderly English butler, who has worked in Lord Darlington's large country house for most of his life. When Lord Darlington dies, the house is bought by an American, and Stevens stays on as his butler. As he gets older, however, he begins to wonder if he has wasted his life. He discovers feelings which, up to now, he has never allowed himself to express.

At the moment Stevens is taking a short motoring holiday in the south-west of England, and is staying in Weymouth, a seaside town. He is sitting on a bench when a stranger joins him, and they start a conversation. Stevens tells the stranger he is a butler in a grand house, and even passes on some of his professional secrets.

Before you read

1 What do you think the title, *The Remains of the Day*, means? Choose **a**, **b**, **c** or **d**.

   a an evening meal   **b** leftover food   **c** what's left of life   **d** a ruined castle

2 Do you think a butler working in a large country house would have an easy or a difficult life? Why? What would he have to do?

Now read to the end of the text.

Think about these questions as you read. Is the text …

… exciting?   … funny?   … difficult?   … scary?   … sad?   … interesting?

As I say, my companion seemed genuinely interested, but after a time I felt I had revealed enough and so concluded by saying:

'Of course, things are quite different today under my present employer. An American gentleman.'

'American, eh? Well, they're the only ones can afford it now. So you stayed on with the house. Part of the package.' He turned and gave me a grin.

'Yes,' I said, laughing a little. 'As you say, part of the package.'

The man turned his gaze back to the sea again, took a deep breath and sighed contentedly. We then proceeded to sit there together quietly for several moments.

'The fact is, of course,' I said after a while, 'I gave my best to Lord Darlington. I gave him the very best I had to give, and now – well – I find I do not have a great deal more left to give.'

The man said nothing, but nodded, so I went on:

'Since my new employer Mr Farraday arrived, I've tried very hard, very hard indeed, to provide the sort of service I would like him to have. I've tried and tried, but whatever I do I find I am far from reaching the standards I once set myself. More and more errors are appearing in my work. Quite trivial in themselves – at least so far. But they're of the sort I would never have made before, and I know what they signify. Goodness knows, I've tried and tried, but it's no use. I've given what I had to give. I gave it all to Lord Darlington.'

'Oh dear, mate. Here, you want a hankie? I've got one somewhere. Here we are. It's fairly clean. Just blew my nose once this morning, that's all. Have a go, mate.'

'Oh dear, no, thank you, it's quite all right. I'm very sorry, I'm afraid the travelling has tired me. I'm very sorry.'

'You must have been very attached to this Lord whatever. And it's three years since he passed away, you say? I can see you were very attached to him, mate.'

'Lord Darlington wasn't a bad man. He wasn't a bad man at all. And at least he had the privilege of being able to say at the end of his life that he made his own mistakes. His lordship was a courageous man. He chose a certain path in life, it proved to be a misguided one, but there, he chose it, he can say that at least. As for myself, I cannot even claim that. You see, I *trusted*. I trusted in his lordship's wisdom. All those years I served him, I trusted I was doing something worthwhile. I can't even say I made my own mistakes. Really – one has to ask oneself – what dignity is there in that?'

'Now, look, mate, I'm not sure I follow everything you're saying. But if you ask me, your attitude's all wrong, see? Don't keep looking back all the time, you're bound to get depressed. And all right, you can't do your job as well as you used to. But it's the same for all of us, see? We've all got to put our feet up at some point. Look at me. Been happy as a lark since the day I retired. All right, so neither of us are exactly in our first flush of youth, but you've got to keep looking forward.' And I believe it was then that he said: 'You've got to enjoy yourself. The evening's the best part of the day. You've done your day's work. Now you can put your feet up and enjoy it. That's how I look at it. Ask anybody, they'll all tell you. The evening's the best part of the day.'

Notes

genuinely (line 1): really, honestly
revealed enough (line 2): told enough secrets
concluded (line 2): finished
package (line 6): (here) when you buy several things included in one price
grin (line 6): smile
gaze (line 8): fixed look
errors (line 17): mistakes
trivial (line 17): unimportant
signify (line 19): mean
mate (line 21): (informal) friend
hankie (line 21): (short form) a handkerchief
have a go (line 22): (here) do it, use it
attached to (line 25): fond of
passed away (line 26): died
privilege (line 28): (here) an advantage
courageous (line 29): brave
misguided (line 30): wrong
dignity (line 33): the quality of being respected by other people
bound to (line 35): sure to, certain to
put our feet up (line 37): relax, stop work
retired (line 38): stopped work and lived on a pension
in our first flush of youth (line 38): very young

Working with the text

Do you like the text? Why or why not?

A Answer the questions.

1 Why does Stevens stop talking about his professional secrets?
2 What does the stranger think about Americans in general?
3 What sad fact does Stevens state in lines 10–12?
4 Why does the stranger offer Stevens a handkerchief? Is it a clean one?
5 Is Lord Darlington alive or dead? How do you know?
6 According to Stevens, what was Lord Darlington's best quality?
7 What does Stevens think is the difference between himself and Lord Darlington?
8 How does the stranger feel about retirement? What expression does he use to show his feeling?
9 What is the stranger's advice to Stevens?

B True or false? Tick (✔) any true sentences and rewrite the false ones.

1 Stevens used to work for an American, Mr Farraday.
2 Lord Darlington gave his best to Stevens.
3 Stevens never makes mistakes in his work.
4 The stranger feels sorry for Stevens.
5 Stevens thinks he has lost his dignity.
6 The stranger understands everything Stevens says.

C Match the adjectives (1–5) to the nouns (a–e) to make pairs of words from the text. Try to do it from memory, then check with the text.

1 present   a errors
2 deep   b path
3 trivial   c employer
4 clean   d breath
5 certain   e hankie

D Reading between the lines

1 Why do you think the stranger 'sighed contentedly' (line 8)? Think of two possible reasons.
2 Why do you think Stevens refuses to borrow the stranger's handkerchief? How do you think he feels about crying in public? Is he really crying because the travelling has tired him?

E Discussion

1 When Stevens talks of 'giving his best' to Lord Darlington, what do you think he means? Should you always 'give your best' to your employer?
2 Why do you think Stevens says Lord Darlington's path in life was 'misguided' (line 30)? Imagine what Lord Darlington did that was wrong.
3 How important do you think the idea of 'dignity' is for Stevens, and why? Is it because of his character, his age, his job, or something else?
4 What is your opinion of the stranger's advice? What is the most important part of it for Stevens?

The Remains of the Day

5 What do you think the stranger means when he says, 'The evening's the best part of the day' (line 40)? Do you agree with him?

F Prediction

What do you think happens next? Tick (✔) as many as you like. Stevens ...

a retires soon after.
b finds happiness with a woman friend.
c tries not to look back to the past so much.
d loses his job with Mr Farraday.
e starts his own business.

What would you *like* to happen next?

Language work

A 'I've tried very hard' (line 14). *Hard* is an irregular adverb. Here are some other adverbs. Match the adverbs to the verbs below.

> well   far away   fast   straight on
> late   nearby

> live   walk   arrive   cook
> work   drive

Make sentences using a different adverb and verb each time.

B 'Been happy as a lark' (line 38). *A lark* is a bird which sings beautifully, very high in the sky. The stranger uses this expression to show Stevens that he has been extremely happy. Match these parts of well-known expressions.

1 good   a as night
2 white   b as houses
3 black   c as a sheet
4 light   d as a picture
5 pretty   e as gold
6 safe   f as a feather

Now choose three of these, and think of situations where you could say them.

C '... you've got to keep looking forward' (line 39). *Keep* means *continue* and is followed by the gerund or *-ing* form. Some of the verbs in the box take the gerund, some take the infinitive. Tick (✔) the ones which take the gerund.

> mind   offer   decide   enjoy   promise
> manage   avoid   hope

Now look at the sentences, and put the verb in brackets in the correct form – gerund or infinitive.

1 Would you mind (help) me with my homework?
2 He promised (give) me the job, so I think he should keep his word.
3 I really enjoyed (spend) the evening round at Tom's house.
4 The company hopes (take on) more workers soon.
5 We offered (lend) Pete our digital camera for his holiday.
6 I only just avoided (bump) into a parked car.

Role play

Student A: You've just started a new job and you're in a real panic about it. However hard you try (and you're doing a lot of overtime!), you keep making mistakes and getting things wrong. There seems so much to learn. You're beginning to feel it's too difficult for you, and you may have to leave. Tell your friend (Student B) how worried you are about it.

Student B: You've often seen your friend (Student A) get in a panic before, and you know he or she worries far too much. Try to calm your friend down. Explain that it isn't his or her fault, but the boss's, for not giving enough training and support. Say that it will soon become easier, especially if the company provides some help.

Writing

Imagine you are Stevens. You have finished your motoring holiday and are back at work. Write a card (35–45 words) to the man you talked to in Weymouth. In your card:

- explain where you are now
- thank him for his advice
- say if you have taken his advice or not.

INDEX TO EXERCISES

Numbers are unit numbers.

Grammar

Adverbs, irregular	19, 28
Adverbs, regular	7, 23
Articles	2
Comparative adjectives	1
Countables & uncountables	7
First conditional	3, 8
For & *since*	5
Gerund & infinitive	18, 20, 28
Give, etc. + indirect object	4
Going to	12
Imperative	12
Indirect questions	11
Linking words	21, 23
Might	2
Modals	4
Must (probability)	3
Past continuous	3
Past perfect	25
Past simple, irregular	11, 17
Past simple passive	15, 24
Possessive apostrophe	27
Present continuous	22
Present continuous (future)	15
Present perfect	19, 22
Present simple	5
Present simple passive	15
Question-words	1, 21
Reflexive pronouns	18
Relative pronouns	16, 27
Reported speech	24
Second conditional	9
So that	20
Superlative adjectives	26
Unless	2
Used to	13
When, etc. + present simple	22
Will (prediction, promises)	5

Vocabulary

Collocations	10
Court-room words	23
Family words	14
Food and cooking words	6
House and home words	17
Odd one out	15
Phrasal verbs	8, 20, 25
Practically	9
Prepositions after adjectives	17
Prepositions after verbs	13, 25
Prepositions of place	6
Quietness & noise	26

Expressions

After, over, in, to, from, by	27
All you have to do	10
As deaf as a post, etc.	16
As happy as a lark, etc.	28
At	4
By	10

Other

Exaggeration	26
Riddles	7
Sarcasm	14
Secret code	14

Writing

A diary entry	5
An e-mail	2, 18, 19, 26
A letter	8, 9, 20, 23
A message	24
A postcard	1, 10, 22, 28
A story	4, 7, 13, 15, 17

Key

Note to the teacher

In any exercise headed *Prediction* which is about the next text, students should discuss the alternatives available and choose the one(s) they think are most probable. Try to avoid giving them the answer(s); this should motivate them to read the text to find out if they were right. However, in any *Prediction* exercise about the rest of the story or book, you can give the answers to your students, once they have discussed all the alternatives and made their choices. It would also be a good idea to encourage students to get the book and read the rest of the story for themselves. The answers are given in the Key.

1 CHRIS STEWART

Before you read

1 **b** is correct.
2 **b** and **c** are correct.

Working with the text

A 1h 2g 3f 4b 5a 6d 7j 8e 9c 10i

B 1 With Pedro and Maria, at El Valero.
2 The fields, as the sun is going down, and the fruit and vegetables growing there.
3 Chris does. He is referring to El Valero.
4 There is no road for cars to the farmhouse.
5 There is a long and rather difficult walk across the valley to the farm.
6 Excited at the thought of seeing it together.

C 1T
2F Ana has *not* seen the farm before.
3F The cabbages and potatoes *don't* belong to Chris.
4F The farm can *only be seen at certain places* along the road.
5F Ana is *not* generally an enthusiastic person.
6T

D 1 He means it is small and light; it makes a tinny noise when he drives it. He doesn't like it.
2 He is proud of having discovered such a beautiful place, where fruit and vegetables like these can grow so well.
3 He is a little nervous and hopes she will like it as much as he does. He asks worriedly, 'What do you think?'
4 For Ana, who can be very critical, this comment is high praise.

E tricky walk, huge eucalyptus, evening breeze, steep bed, new home

F d, c, b, e, a

H **d** and **e** are correct.

Language work

A 1 more beautiful
2 more enthusiastic
3 nicer
4 longer

B 1 *What* colour are the mountain peaks? Rose pink.
2 *What* is Suspiro del Moro? A way through the mountains of the Sierra Nevada. or *Where* is Suspiro del Moro? In the Sierra Nevada.
3 *Who* are the farm's previous owners? Pedro and Maria.
4 *What* kinds of fruit are growing along the road? Olives, oranges and lemons.
5 *Where* do Chris and Ana park the car? Where the road runs out.
6 *Where* exactly are the birds singing? In a group of large eucalyptus trees.

2 ALEXANDER MCCALL SMITH

Before you read

1 **d** is correct.
2 Precious's parents probably gave her this name because they loved her very much; she was very important to them.
3 [*Note to teachers:* **c** is correct, but it is better not to give students this answer. They will find it out as they work through the unit.]

Working with the text

A 1 He is sitting in a chair outside Happy's front door.
2 He gives a cry of surprise and sadness.
3 No.
4 He offers to pay for some blood (probably with Happy's money).

129

Key

B 1 She is pretending to come straight from the hospital in order to save Happy's life.
2 He doesn't want to work, and doesn't need to, as long as Happy pays for everything.
3 Because Happy has a good job and a nice house, and because he can have an easy, comfortable life as her father.
4 She is pretending to be in a great hurry, as this is an emergency.
5 She prefers to trust Happy's feeling that he isn't her father.
6 By asking him to risk his life to save his daughter's. When he refuses to help, he shows that he isn't Happy's father. Any parent would want to give blood to save their child's life.

C 1e 2g 3b 4a 5h 6d 7f 8c

D d, f, e, b, a, c

F **b**, **c** and **e** are correct.

Language work

A 1d 2a 3b 4e 5c

B 1 might damage it
2 might catch cold
3 might come
4 might hurt
5 might get
6 might see

C 1 an 2 a 3 a 4 an, a 5 a 6 an 7 a 8 an 9 a 10 an 11 a 12 an 13 an 14 a 15 a

[*Note to teachers:* people used to say *an history book, an historian,* but this is now considered old-fashioned.]

3 Ernest Hemingway

Before you read

1 **a** is correct.
2 **b** and **d** are correct.

Working with the text

A 1 In a north-westerly direction.
2 A very large fish.
3 4 o'clock in the afternoon.
4 A straw hat.
5 A bottle of water.
6 The fishing boat is far out in the ocean.
7 The fish.
8 By looking at the position of the stars.

B 1 To help him, because the old man is afraid he isn't strong enough to hold on to the fish.
2 The fish might break the line.
The fish might dive down and take the boat with him.
3 He is using the weight of his body to hold on to the fishing line.
4 He is impressed by the fish's strength and size.
5 He feels tired, because he 'rested against the bow'.
6 *Possible answer:* 'It will be easy for me to sail into my home port, using the lights of Havana to show me the way.'
7 He wants to see the fish, at least once before he or the fish dies.

C 1T
2T
3F The fish is swimming *away from the coast/out to sea*.
4F The old man drinks some *water*.
5F The old man plans to *use the lights of Havana to sail home*.
6F After the sun goes down, it is a *cold* night.

E 1a, 2b and 3b are correct.

Language work

A 1f 2c 3e 4a 5d 6b

B 1 It *was raining* quite hard while we *were shopping* this morning.
2 Natalie *was talking* all the time I *was trying* to do my homework.
3 The guards *weren't listening* to the prisoners, who *were planning* their escape.
4 I *was drinking* my coffee and *(was) reading* the newspaper.
5 *Were you singing* while you *were having* your bath?
6 No one *was listening* to the woman while she *was telling* her story.
7 Two hours later I *was still driving* and the boys *were still sleeping* in the back of the car.
8 I *wasn't watching* TV just then – I *was doing* my homework!

C 1d 2f 3a 4c 5b 6e

4 John Grisham

Before you read

Any of these answers, if there are good reasons for choosing them.

Working with the text

A 1c 2b 3d 4a

B 1 The woman hides in *an airport lounge for an hour*.
2 She drinks expensive *water*.
3 She buys a one-way ticket to *São Paulo*.
4 Her home *isn't* in São Paulo.
5 She wants to be closer to her *father*.

C 1 Brazil.
2 No, she doesn't, because she says 'wherever he was'; that means she doesn't know where he is.

130

KEY

D **a** is correct.

E 1 Customs and immigration personnel, and the airlines.
2 Once they know her father's identity, they can find her name by looking up details of his family on their computer records.
3 She is only worried about the men who are following her.
4 He presses an alarm button at his desk.
5 When she sees the other travellers moving fast through the checkpoints, while she herself is being held up.
6 She has no choice. The supervisor has her passport and there is a uniformed guard beside him.

F 1e 2c 3a 4f 5d 6b

G 1 It sounds like a Spanish name, but he doesn't look Hispanic.
2 She is annoyed at being questioned.
3 She is really Eva Miranda.

I **a** and **c** are correct.

Language work

A 1 mustn't 2 may 3 Would 4 don't have to
5 should 6 can

B 1 At least 2 at night 3 at once
4 at the most 5 at the moment
6 at her best 7 at last 8 at all

C 1 Please pass me the salt./Pass me the salt please.
2 Can you give him a message?
3 I'll send you the photos by e-mail.
4 Could you possibly bring us the menu?
5 I'll show you the plants you could buy.
6 The lawyer handed her the documents to sign.
7 When I visited her in hospital, I took her some flowers.

5 SUE TOWNSEND

Before you read

a and **c** are correct.

Working with the text

A 1 A green lurex apron.
2 The family dog was shut out of the house, and it barked all night outside Adrian's window.
3 He thinks that it is a boil, and that everybody will notice it.
4 He thinks the whole family has a very poor diet, with not enough vitamins.
5 Adrian's mother didn't close the gate when the dog was outside the house.
6 Adrian has broken the arm of the stereo (used for playing records).

B 1d 2e 3g 4c 5b 6a 7h 8f

C 1 unhelpful, untidy, unkind – for example.
2 Because she hasn't worn the green lurex apron he gave her this year.
3 He is worried that lack of vitamin C is causing his spots. He thinks his mother should provide better meals for the family. His mother doesn't appear to feel guilty.
4 Then no one will notice that Adrian has broken the arm of the stereo.
5 'Just my luck!' means 'I'm always so unlucky!'
  a He has a spot on his face for the beginning of the year.
  b The dog barked outside Adrian's window all night.
  c The spot is on Adrian's chin, just where everyone can see it.

E **a**, **b** and **d** are correct.

F 1F Adrian's teachers are *not* impressed by his intelligence.
2F Adrian falls in love with Pandora *after a day or two*.
3T
4F Adrian has *two* aspirins at midday.

G 1 He wants to improve his skin and get rid of his spots.
2 His mother is always talking about it, and he thinks it will show that he's an intellectual.
3 They were having a private conversation.
4 She is angry because she, not her husband, has to clean the drains, and also because her husband is drinking coffee with Mrs Mole.
5 In Ancient Greek mythology, Pandora was the first woman on earth. She was given a box and told not to open it, but she disobeyed and opened the box. Adrian's friend Pandora uses the name 'Box' as a sort of intellectual joke.
6 She can't because she is carrying big bags of shopping.
7 No, because no girl likes being told her eyes are like a dog's, and a mongrel is usually the least attractive kind of dog.
8 She should buy more fruit and vegetables for the family to eat.
9 Pandora starts going out with Nigel.
10 He hates Nigel and would like him to die a painful death.

I **a** and **c** are correct.

Language work

A 1 since 2 for 3 since 4 for 5 for 6 Since

B 1 I think the weather will probably be fine tomorrow.
2 I know you will/you'll be very happy together.
3 I promise I will/I'll help you as much as I can.
4 I'm sure there will/there'll be no problems on the journey.
5 I don't think I will/I'll be able to attend the wedding.
6 I have a feeling nobody will/nobody'll come to my party!

C 1 face, see 2 crosses, runs 3 visit, enjoy
4 lies, rises 5 pick, eat, sell

131

KEY

6 Frank McCourt

Before you read

a is correct.

Working with the text

A 1 When Mr McCourt gets a job, and especially when he brings home his wages.
2 No.
3 Mrs McCourt boils water and washes the children; Mr McCourt dries them. They drink hot cocoa and stay up while their father invents a story to tell them.
4 a Eggs, fried tomatoes, fried bread, tea with sugar and milk.
b Mashed potatoes, peas, ham and trifle.
5 She is worried about it, and thinks it is bad for him.
6 Mr McCourt does not bring home his wages.

B 1 A love song.
2 She uses credit; she promises to pay in future, when she has some money.
3 She only does the housework when she is really happy and relaxed, and that is when her husband brings home his wages.
4 She is very proud, and doesn't want anyone to see how old and worn her family's clothes are.
5 Once a week, on Saturday night.
6 Very worried and depressed.

C 1h 2e 3a 4j 5i 6d 7b 8g 9f 10c

D 1e 2d 3a 4c 5f 6b

F **a** is correct. In fact, Frank's father has spent all his wages on buying drinks for himself and his friends.

Language work

A 1 at 2 in 3 in 4 on 5 to 6 at 7 on 8 to

B 1 milk 2 Fried 3 salt 4 Eggs 5 bread, butter

Role play

[Note to teachers: used to is a useful structure here. For example: When I was eight, my parents used to send me to my room if I was naughty!]

7 Lewis Carroll

Before you read

b is correct.

Working with the text

A 1 Three.
2 All the things needed for tea (cups, saucers, plates, teapot, etc.).
3 He offers her some wine, but there isn't any.
4 He says her hair needs cutting, which she thinks is a rude thing to say.
5 She enjoys riddles and thinks she can guess the answer.

B 1ai, bii; 2aii, bi; 3ai, bii; 4aii, bi; 5ai, bii

C 1F The March Hare and his friends think there is *no room* for Alice.
2F The table is laid for *many more than* three people to have tea.
3F The Hatter *doesn't like* Alice's long hair.
4T

D 1 He is mad, but he's also trying to tell her that it was wrong of her to sit down without being invited.
2 He is shocked at being criticised by Alice.
3 The Hatter is pointing out that the Dormouse spends almost all his time sleeping, so that whenever he is breathing, he is sleeping. The conversation stops here because they have run out of things that 'you might just as well say'.

F 1 The Hatter continues the conversation.
2 Alice tries to understand a story told by the Dormouse.
3 The March Hare offers Alice some tea.

Language work

A *Uncountable:* bread, meat, furniture, water, news, fruit, information, advice, sugar.
Countable: book, letter, car, chair, people, vegetable.
1 is 2 was 3 is 4 come 5 looks 6 smells

B 1 slowly 2 happily 3 sadly 4 easily 5 Suddenly 6 hungrily

C 1 A bottle.
2 When it has turned into a garage.
3 One minds the train and the other trains the mind.
4 So that he could make a clean getaway.
5 Because he had no body to go with.
6 I don't know and I don't care!

8 David Hempleman-Adams

Before you read

Any of these answers, if there are good reasons for choosing them.

Working with the text

A 1b 2h 3f 4i 5a 6l 7k 8j 9e 10d 11g 12c

B 1 15 years.
2 He falls through the ice into the water. He did not notice that the ice was too thin to stand on.

132

KEY

3 He pulls his ice-spikes from around his neck (where he carries them), tries to dig them into some thicker ice, and calls to Rune for help.
4 He is a poor swimmer. He says swimming 'is something I find difficult at the best of times'.
5 He thinks he is going to die.
6 He is worried that frostbite will spread over his body and they will have to give up their attempt on the North Pole.

C 1 Falling into the freezing water and being unable to get out.
2 He thinks Rune won't hear him, and he (David) will drown.
3 He is in front, and cannot see much in the white-out.
4 Very close. He could drown, or die of the cold.

E 1 hauling me out
2 double-quick
3 sodden clothing
4 The best thing you can do is
5 It sounds unlikely
6 terrified

F 1F Rune *pulls David out of the water*.
2F David's *trouser legs* are frozen solid.
3T
4T
5F David accepts his friend's advice *in the end*.
6T

G 1 David probably has the impression that being in the water lasts a long time.
2 To get warm and to recover from his experience.

I **b** is correct.

Language work

A 1c help, we will/we'll get
2d is, I will/I'll phone
3a We will/We'll eat, is
4e I will/I'll have, is
5b I will not/I won't go, am

B 1 taking off   2 call for   3 look after   4 look up
5 has grown up

9 ROBERT HARRIS

Before you read

a and **d** are correct.
'Enigma' actually means a puzzle or mystery which is difficult to solve, and it was the name of a German code machine.

Working with the text

A 1c 2b 3a 4a

B 1c 2i 3a 4h 5b 6g 7f 8e 9d

C 1 Claire Romilly.
2 Wigram wanted to get information from Tom about Claire.
3 Claire.
4 The authorities think it is essential to find her quickly.
5 Wigram. He wants a photo of Claire to help the police in their search for her.
6 Perhaps she is a spy who has given secret information to the enemy. If she is caught, she could be sentenced to death.

D 1 No. He leaves his dirty clothes on the bed 'more in hope than expectation'.
2 They are paying guests – people who pay to live in Mrs Armstrong's house. They each have a room; Mrs Armstrong cooks their meals and (sometimes) does their washing.
3 Tom finds the other guests uninteresting. The toast is made with old bread, and the tea is not strong enough.
4 *Possible answer:* The radio news says that the Russian army is defending a city called Kharkov (in the Ukraine) against German attack.
5 Miss Quince.
6 Mr Noakes.
7 An envelope. It was delivered by hand, not by the postman.

E 1 Tom is depressed and unhappy, because he is worried about Claire's disappearance.
2 He is bored by the other guests' conversation, and he does not want them to guess how he feels.

G 1d, 2a and 3b are correct.

Language work

A 1d 2a 3f 4b 5c 6e

B 1 I practically crashed the car.
2 She practically fell over.
3 He practically broke his leg.
4 I could practically see the finishing line.
5 Her little son could practically read when he was two!

10 ANNE TYLER

Before you read

b and **d** are correct.

Working with the text

A 1 He dreamt his son was alive but then remembers that he is dead.
2 The new book Macon is writing for his publisher.
3 August 3rd.
4 August 31st.

B 1b 2d 3a 4c

133

KEY

C 1 He dreams of Ethan because he wishes his son were alive. He feels extremely sad about Ethan's death. We know this because 'there was a thud of disappointment somewhere inside his rib cage' and 'He understood why people said hearts "sank"'.
2 To find out when the manuscript will be ready.
3 Julian likes the fact that Macon is very different from other people, and he enjoys making gentle fun of Macon. We know he is fond of Macon because he is understanding about Macon's reluctance to finish the book, and gives him more time to complete it.
4 *Macon:* quiet, slow-moving.
Julian: carefree, energetic, cheerful, businesslike, enthusiastic.

E 1a, 2c and 3a are correct.

Language work

A 1e   2d   3a   4b   5c

B 1 All you have to do is (to) press the green button.
2 All you have to do is (to) type your name in.
3 All you have to do is (to) renew your passport.
4 All you have to do is (to) buy some vegetables (on your way here).
5 All you have to do is (to) ring the garage.

C 1c   2e   3d   4f   5a   6b

11 SEBASTIAN FAULKS

Before you read

Any of these answers, if there are good reasons for choosing them.

Working with the text

A 1 To bring out the dead body of Jack Firebrace.
2 The sunshine is too bright for them after the darkness of the tunnel.
3 The war has just ended.
4 Four years.
5 Very sad, and not sure what to do next.

B 1c 2f 3h 4b 5i 6g 7e 8a 9d

C 1 He can hardly believe he has survived. He needs time to adjust his thoughts.
2 The thick line of German troops (like a dam) has been broken; they have retreated.
3 Friends of Stephen's, men who had fought with him. They both died at Thiepval, where large numbers of British soldiers were killed.
4 Men fighting in France spent a lot of time in underground trenches, which sometimes looked like rabbits' burrows.
5 'Him' refers to Stephen. The sentence refers to a previous battle in which thousands of men died, including Byrne.
6 He is sad at the death of his friends and all the other soldiers. He does not know what to do with the rest of his life. He is relieved to be alive.

D **a**, **b** and **c** are correct.

E 1 Now that the war is over, Jack and Joseph can be buried together, as they are no longer enemies, but both victims of the fighting.
2 They are all thinking of the waste of life, of the men they have known who are dead now.
3 He is saying goodbye to them.
4 He is almost expecting to be shot by the enemy.
5 A kiss feels like a touch on the skin; Stephen thinks the bullets might feel like that.
6 Exhausted but full of joy.

F 1 He is very fond of Stephen, because he (Levi) is so glad to have saved Stephen's life.
2 To show that they are friends, and to remember each other in future.
3 War has stopped, and no one is hurting or harming anyone else.

G 1c   2a   3f   4b   5e   6d

H foot

Language work

A 1 caught 2 Did 3 did that happen 4 Didn't you hear 5 fell 6 pulled 7 had to

B 1 He did not know what he could do.
2 She wondered how long she should wait.
3 I didn't understand what they were saying.
4 I asked her if I could leave early.
5 I asked if there was any more information.

12 DODIE SMITH

Before you read

[*Note to teachers:* **e** is correct, but it is better not to give students this answer. They will find it out as they work through the unit.]

Working with the text

A 1g 2f 3a 4c 5d 6h 7e 8b

B 1 The steps lead up to a doorway into the tower; they are outside the tower.
2 It is used for climbing down to the ground, inside the tower.
3 Inside the tower.
4 Cassandra and Thomas.
5 He thinks Thomas is at school.
6 A mattress on an old iron bedstead, with blankets and pillows on it, attractive new stationery on a rustic table, with stones to hold the paper down, the kitchen arm-chair, washing arrangements and drinking water.

134

7 In order to make him do some writing.

C 1 To see if repairs to the tower are needed.
2 Because he sees the bed, table and chair there; they have been put there for him!
3 She means that *he* is going to be camping out there (sleeping and eating in the tower).
4 She is afraid he may have become mad, because they have shut him in the tower.
5 a He thinks it's very funny. He laughs loudly.
   b He is very angry. He shouts at Thomas and Cassandra to bring back the ladder.

D 1 oak   2 ladder   3 crumbling   4 mattress
5 lantern   6 Thermos

E c, e, b, d, a

G 1a and 2c are correct.

Language work

A 1 are going to
2 is going to
3 are going to
4 are going to
5 am going to

B 1 switch   2 Bring   3 Hold   4 sit   5 take   6 Listen

13 J.R.R. TOLKIEN

Before you read

1 **a** is correct.
2 **b** is correct.
3 **b** is correct.

Working with the text

A 1c   2a   3g   4b   5d   6h   7e   8f

B 1 Excited and happy.
2 Some dwarves.
3 No, just to Gandalf.
4 Frodo Baggins.
5 Do not use it. Keep it secret, and keep it safe.

C 1 sniffing   2 present   3 off   4 mantelpiece
5 master, ring

D 1 He has done this before, because he says, 'What fun to be off *again*!' So it isn't his first journey.
2 To take care of himself, to keep away from danger.
3 He isn't worried about any danger, or about looking after himself.
4 It will be a long journey, and he doesn't know exactly where he will go.
5 He does expect to see Bilbo again, because he says, 'Good-bye, my dear Bilbo – *until our next meeting!*'
6 Frodo is very fond of Bilbo and is sorry that Bilbo has gone. He is also sorry that he did not see Bilbo off.

7 Frodo knew that Bilbo had a magic ring, because he says, 'The ring! Has he left me that?' If he didn't know about it, he would say, 'A ring? Has he left me one?'

F 1a, 2a and 2c are correct.

Language work

B 1c You're going too fast – wait *for* me!
2e We spent a long time talking *about* Angela's problems.
3f I was told to ask *for* the manager – is he in?
4b Shall we go out? It depends *on* the weather, doesn't it?
5d I always disagree *with* Tom – his ideas are crazy!
6a Why is he laughing *at* me? What's so funny?

14 GRAHAM GREENE

Before you read

A codebook, invisible ink, a good camera, a hand gun and notebooks.

Working with the text

A 1 He thinks it is better if only he and Rudy know the combination (Beatrice knew the previous combination).
2 Because Wormold tells her she is making him nervous.
3 She means that he hasn't actually remembered it, and that he is not very good at remembering anything.
4 She has been dead for fifteen years.
5 It is made up of five numbers; there are too many combinations of five numbers to try them all, or guess the right one.

B 1c   2a   3e   4b   5d

C 1 He wants to give her the impression that he knows all about the work of intelligence agents and is thoroughly professional in his approach to spying.
2 Rudy knows the combination to open the safe.

D 1F Beatrice is *slightly rude* to her boss, Wormold.
2F Beatrice *says* that the combination of the safe *seems* secure.
3F Wormold and Beatrice *don't* phone Oxford for help.
4F Great-aunt Kate is *not* a secret agent.
5F Beatrice is *not* impressed with Wormold's efficiency.

F 1a, 2a and 3c are correct.

Language work

A 1e   2h   3a   4f   5b   6c   7d   8g

[*Note to teachers:* your brother-in-law can also be your sister's husband.]

B 1 Oh wonderful!
2 That's really great.
3 Thanks a lot!

135

KEY

4 Poor woman – however will she manage!
5 Another lovely day!

C *Message:* I need a gun. *Code:* use numbers for the alphabet plus one, so that A=2, B=3, C=4, etc.

15 LAURIE LEE

Before you read

e is correct.

Working with the text

A 1 There were only two classes in the school, one for younger pupils and one for older ones.
2 One or two.
3 About ten years, until they were fourteen years old.
4 Some historical facts, and a rough idea of world geography.
5 Four years old.
6 Some of the children stole it.

B 1f 2g 3a 4c 5d 6e 7b

C 1g 2a 3i 4b 5j 6l 7f 8e 9k 10d 11h 12c

D 1 It was enough for country children.
2 The education that country children received at the village school was more than their grandparents ever had the chance of getting (in the past, school was not compulsory).
3 'At its peak' means that the school had the largest number of children in its history. 'Universal education' means that all children have to go to school, by law.
4 They came from houses and farms in distant places, far from the more civilised towns and villages.
5 In this text there do not appear to be any boys or men in Laurie's family – 'the womanly warmth of my family'. (In fact, he does have brothers, and an absent father.)
6 It was autumn or winter, because it was cold enough for Laurie to be wrapped up in scarves.
7 He did not want to go, because he knew nothing about school.
8 They were trying to frighten him into doing what they told him. He realised it wasn't true, but it made him keep quiet for a while.
9 He was bullied by the older children, and he didn't like it.

F **a** is correct.

Language work

A 1 boots (worn on the legs or feet)
2 elbow (not part of the face or head)
3 standing (not moving)
4 ain't (the only ungrammatical word)
5 cheese (not a vegetable or fruit)

[*Note to teachers:* students might be able to make a case for other odd ones out.]

B 1 made 2 spoken 3 kept 4 cut 5 won
6 given

C 1 am having, are coming
2 Are you doing
3 are seeing
4 am booking, am buying
5 is repairing
6 is arriving, am meeting

16 MURRAY BAIL

Before you read

b and **c** are correct.

Working with the text

A 1g 2a 3f 4b 5e 6c 7d

B e, c, b, d, f, a

C 1 She is a little angry with him.
2 He wants to try out different expressions, and to see what he looks like to other people.
3 He feels quite excited and happy to be doing something different. His wife does realise this.

E 1 No.
2 Because of his job as a piano-tuner.
3 To march backwards and forwards, to look after equipment and learn when to salute.

F 1 stand 2 brief 3 stamp 4 hold

G 1 That Australia has no chance of winning the war if all its soldiers are as useless as Banerjee.
2 He is disappointed.
3 Artists and musicians, as well as people physically incapable of fighting.

H 1c and 2b are correct.

Language work

A 1d 2e 3d 4b 5a

B 1f a garden where there hasn't been any rain
2d a very boring person
3a a completely crazy person
4b something that is very clear or obvious
5c a very simple thing to do
6e a country with no hills

[*Note to teachers:* in Unit 7, the expression *as mad as a hatter* is explained.]

136

KEY

17 SUSAN HILL

[*Note to teachers:* there is a famous novel with a similar title, *The Woman in White*, written by William Wilkie Collins and published in 1860. It is a Victorian classic, the first and probably the greatest 'sensation' novel. A man's meeting with a strange woman dressed in white draws him into a story of crime, poison, kidnapping and murder. Susan Hill's novel is also about a man meeting a strange woman in a lonely place, and the effect this meeting has on his life, but *The Woman in Black* is a ghost story.]

Before you read

a and **f** are correct.

Working with the text

A 1d 2f 3h 4g 5b 6c 7e 8a

B 1F *Moonlight* is coming through the window.
    2F The window is *slightly ajar*.
    3F Arthur *doesn't realise at first* why he has woken up.
    4T
    5F The faint noise sounds *quite near*.
    6F Arthur gets up and goes into the corridor *after some time*.
    7T
    8F The door at the end of the passage is *shut and locked*.

C 1 He is suddenly afraid, because he realises that Spider is aware of something or someone in the house.
    2 Arthur feels that something terrible is about to happen.
    3 Spider can feel an evil presence nearby.
    4 Nothing else happens and he has the dog as a companion.
    5 Very frightened, only just brave enough to open the door.
    6 Spider knows that the evil/the enemy/the ghost is in that room.

D 1f 2d 3a 4c 5h 6g 7b 8e

F **a** is correct.

Language work

A 1 woke 2 sat 3 heard 4 was/felt 5 got
    6 took 7 had 8 found/saw 9 came
    10 knew/thought/realised

B *Bathroom:* toilet, cupboard, bath, shower, basin
    Kitchen: fridge, dishwasher, microwave, freezer, cooker
    Sitting room: television, stereo, fireplace, piano, sofa

[*Note to teachers:* cupboard could also be in the kitchen or the sitting room.]

C 1 of, of 2 about/at/over 3 in 4 by/at 5 with
    6 for 7 of

18 JOHN LE CARRÉ

Before you read

All these answers are correct.

Working with the text

A 1f 2b 3d 4a 5e 6c

B 1 Almost four o'clock in the morning.
    2 No.
    3 Jack Brotherhood is holding her arm. He wants to wait until Harry is ready to plug equipment into the phone, in order to find out who is calling.
    4 No.
    5 No, she doesn't recognise it.
    6 She feels sure it is Magnus calling, and suddenly loses control of herself, because she is very worried about him.
    7 No, the call was too short.

C 1 He thinks Magnus has taken the old photos and mementoes away with him, and may not be coming back.
    2 She is annoyed by Jack's constant questions.
    3 They think it is Magnus. Mary is praying that it will be him, that he will come home and life will return to normal.
    4 She doesn't really think that, but she wants Jack to let her answer the phone.
    5 He wants Harry to have enough time to find out where the call is coming from. Mary knows about 'those games' because she was once trained as a spy herself.
    6 The caller must be a secret agent, but we don't know the caller's nationality.
    7 'With a lover's knowledge'; Jack guesses what Mary is going to do before she does it.
    8 They both want to find Magnus urgently.
    9 She fears Magnus may be a traitor and may have gone to the foreign country he has been spying for.

D 1 Why's this drawer empty?
    2 So what was it full of?
    3 How long's it been empty?
    4 Did he put papers in his suitcase?
    5 Who is that?
    6 Can you hear me?
    7 Who's that calling, please?

E 1d 2c 3a 4e 5g 6b 7f

G **d** is correct.

Language work

A 1 to get 2 cooking 3 looking after 4 writing
    5 going 6 to book 7 watching

B 1 himself 2 yourself 3 myself 4 themselves
    5 ourselves

137

KEY

19 W. Somerset Maugham

Before you read

e is correct.

Working with the text

A 1 breakfast 2 post 3 parcel 4 same 5 surprise 6 copy 7 study

B 1F When they have their meals, the Peregrines sit *at opposite ends of the table*.
2T
3F The colonel *doesn't know* his wife has written a book.
4F The colonel starts reading his newspaper *during breakfast*.
5T

C 1i 2g 3a 4h 5b 6e 7j 8c 9f 10d

D *Evie's good points:* she's a lady, she has some money of her own, she manages the house very well, she's a good hostess, the village people adore her.
Evie's bad points: she hasn't given him any children, she is faded now and no longer pretty.

The colonel's good points: he's a gentleman, he owns a large and comfortable house, he's still a good-looking man, he's an all-round sportsman.
The colonel's bad points: he doesn't like poetry, he is selfish, he blames Evie for not having children.

It seems likely that the colonel has also been a sad disappointment to Evie, because he no longer spends much time with her or shows any interest in her.

F **a**, **c** and **e** are correct.

Language work

A 1 Have the Peregrines ever *been* happy together? Yes, they were probably happy when they were first married.
2 Has Evie ever *written* a book before? No, this is her first.
3 Have the Peregrines *had* any children? No, they haven't.
4 Has the colonel ever *enjoyed* reading poetry? No, he hasn't.
5 Has the colonel ever really *understood* his wife? No, he hasn't.
6 Has the colonel always *thought* more about himself than anyone else? Yes, he has.

B 1 well 2 fast 3 hard 4 late

20 Patricia Highsmith

Before you read

1 **e** is correct.
2 Tom should show feelings of sadness, sympathy and surprise in the letter.

Working with the text

A 1c 2a 3e 4f 5b 6g 7d

B 1 If the Greenleafs think he has had it for a long time, they will wonder why he hasn't told them about it earlier.
2 He needs to appear very surprised, so that nobody will think he had a reason for murdering Dickie.
3 It proves that Dickie planned to be dead by June.
4 If the Greenleafs believe that he has never seen a will before, they won't suspect him of writing this one himself.

C 1f 2d 3e 4b 5a 6c

D [*Note to teachers:* **c** is correct, but it is better not to give students this answer. They will find it out as they work through the unit.]

E 1 He thinks it is a joke.
2 He is delighted.
3 Four Greek policemen who, Tom imagines, will be waiting for him when he arrives on the island of Crete.

F 1 It is an exciting new place to visit.
2 He thinks that, by then, somebody will have realised he murdered Dickie, and the police will arrest him in Crete.
3 *Possible answer:* 'that they were going to arrest him.'
4 Almost wild with happiness. He wants to go to the best hotel, because now he knows he is going to have Dickie's money, and will be a very rich man.

G 1 joke
2 Dickie's money, his freedom
3 everybody
4 imaginary policemen
5 taxi driver

H [*Note to teachers:* if students have seen the 1999 film, ask them how different the film ending is from the one in the book. In the film Tom suddenly feels sorry he has killed Dickie, tells one of Dickie's friends the truth, and then kills him too. It is clear that he cannot escape punishment this time. Ask students to say which ending they prefer and why.]

Language work

A 1e 2f 3h 4c 5g 6i 7j 8b 9d 10a

B 1d Josie saved some money *so that* she could buy a sailing boat.

138

2e I'm giving you the facts *so that* you can decide for yourself.
3b Ed's doing his homework now *so that* he can go out tonight.
4c Jeff's planting some apple trees *so that* one day he can eat his own fruit.
5a Mum's cooking the chicken now *so that* we can eat it cold later.

C 1 watching 2 driving 3 doing 4 collecting
  5 putting

21 LOUIS DE BERNIÈRES

Before you read
a, **b** and **d** are correct.

Working with the text

A 1e 2d 3f 4b 5h 6g 7c 8a

B *Possible answers:*
1 earn his living from playing the mandolin.
2 the war started.
3 is over, he can try to become a professional player.
4 what he thinks is an enormous weasel on his bed. (It's Pelagia's pet pine marten.)
5 she thinks it may be food.
6 is too much for him to bear.
7 he is far from home/he does not understand the Greeks/the Greeks do not like him.
8 Psipsina goes off to look for Pelagia.

C 1b 2c 3b 4a

E 1a and 2c are correct.

Language work

A 1d He passed the test *although* he didn't do much work for it!
  2e I'll have to go to the market *because* we've run out of vegetables.
  3a Jane studied Thai *so that* she could talk to the local people in Bangkok.
  4c We could either eat indoors *or* have a barbecue outside.
  5f Ted went by coach, not train, *in order to* save money.
  6b Come round for coffee *after* you've finished work.

B 1 *Who* wrote *Captain Corelli's Mandolin*? Louis de Bernières.
  2 *When* was it first published? 1994.
  3 *Where* in the world does the story take place? Cephallonia, Greece.
  4 *What* is a mandolin? A musical instrument with strings.
  5 *Whose/Which* bed is Corelli sleeping in? Pelagia's.
  6 *How/What* does the doctor feel about Corelli? He thinks of Corelli as an enemy.

22 CATHERINE CHIDGEY

Before you read
1 **a** is correct.
2 **c** is correct.

Working with the text

A 1c 2d 3a 4f 5b 6e

B 1T
  2F *Patrick's friends* have started a newsletter about him.
  3T
  4F Patrick *can't talk* to his visitors./Patrick's *visitors are talking to him*.
  5T
  6F Patrick is *not* a rich man, *and he needs* his friends' money.
  7F *The Friends of Patrick Mercer want* to know if Colette changes her address.

C 1 He was in a car crash; the car was on fire.
  2 Yes, he did. 'The grafts' and 'the wonderful surgeons' show that he had an operation.
  3 That they are wonderful.
  4 Many experts think that an unconscious person can hear what is being said. If people talk to him or her, it may help the patient to recover consciousness. Letters and tapes may also help, because they show that the patient's friends are thinking of him or her.

E 1 No, she doesn't.
  2 Not really, because she thinks she doesn't know him.
  3 Handwritten.
  4 To see if she has missed something which would explain everything.
  5 On the back of the envelope.
  6 No.
  7 She wants to look more closely at the stamp.
  8 A blurry date.

F 1 She can't understand why the letter is addressed to her.
  2 It only proves that someone has found out Colette's name and her mother's address. It doesn't prove that Colette herself has given her name and address to anyone.
  3 She and Patrick may have been at the same school.
  4 In order to discover the wider world outside New Zealand.

G 1b is correct. [*Note to teachers:* Patrick and Colette's mother had a brief love affair years ago, before Colette was born. Colette's mother told Patrick her name was Colette.]

H **b** is correct.

Language work

A 1d 2c 3a 4e 5b

B 1 have made
  2 have cut, (have) picked

Key

    3 has just driven
    4 have already had
    5 has not learnt
    6 has just fallen

C   1W I'll wait here until the taxi *comes*.
    2C
    3W Read the instructions before you *start* cooking.
    4W I'll check our e-mails while you *unpack* the car.
    5C
    6C

23 Harper Lee

Before you read

c is correct. [*Note to teachers:* Scout is told by her father (and a neighbour) that 'it's a sin to kill a mockingbird'.]

Working with the text

A   1a   2d   3b   4c

B   1c and 2b are correct. [*Note to teachers:* Scout is thinking of one cold February morning when she and all the neighbours were indoors, frightened of a mad dog wandering down the street. The situation was saved by Atticus, who killed the dog with one shot from his gun.]

C   [*Note to teachers:* **b** is correct, but it is better not to give students this answer. They will find it out as they work through the unit.]

D   1c   2e   3d   4a   5b

E   1 That the jury is not looking at Tom Robinson. She knows that a jury doesn't look at a person it has found guilty.
    2 Although her father has defended Tom as well as he could, he hasn't achieved what he wanted. This is like firing a gun with no bullets in it; it won't have any effect.
    3 Shocked and very disappointed.
    4 Disappointed but probably not very surprised.
    5 Either Jem or one of the Negroes. They want her to stand up with them, as her father walks past.

F   1 court-room, jury   2 judge, foreman   3 gavel
    4 lawyers   5 court case   6 convicted

H   **c** is correct.

Language work

A   1e Sonia's going to Peru *in order to* study the Incas.
    2d My sister learnt to drive *and* soon bought a car.
    3b I'll meet you at the café *as soon as* I finish work.
    4a We can't stay at the hotel *because* we haven't got any money!
    5c It was a very hot day *but* nobody was swimming.

B   1 quietly   2 Sadly   3 slowly   4 Stupidly   5 loudly

24 Diana Souhami

Before you read

Any of these answers, if there are good reasons for choosing them.

Working with the text

A   1e   2a   3b   4c   5d

B   1 The ship will sink and the crew will all drown.
    2 Because his advice contradicts (goes against) the captain's orders.
    3 Selkirk says he would rather stay on the island than go to sea in that particular ship.
    4 He didn't realise the argument would have such a serious result. He never thought Stradling would leave him alone on the island.
    5 He can't believe they can leave him to die on the island.
    6 He thinks they are his friends; they are part of his work and his life.
    7 Like a man without a voice.

C   1e   2f   3c   4b   5d   6a

D   **a**, **b** and **c** are correct.

E   1 Between four and five years.
    2 A wooden ship with white sails.
    3 He wants the sailors to land in order to rescue him, but at the same time he doesn't want them to spoil the innocence and beauty of the island.
    4 He hates Stradling as much as ever.
    5 The island is very small.
    6 To welcome sailors to the island; to show that he is on the island.

F   1 He has dreamed of it – 'the ship of his dreams'.
    2 Everything around him looks the same as when Stradling left him on the island in 1704.
    3 He thinks of it as his island. He loves the fact that it is unspoilt. It has kept him alive and he is very grateful to it. He doesn't want the sailors to run all over it, destroying its wildlife and peaceful atmosphere.
    4 He says he doesn't want to see Stradling, but he will probably want to be rescued, even if Stradling is there.

G   [*Note to teachers:* death was the usual punishment for sailors who mutinied.]

H   1d and 2b are correct.

Language work

A   1 was not forgiven
    2 was told
    3 was packed
    4 was left
    5 was pulled up, was towed

B   1 She said (that) the bus could be about fifteen minutes late.

KEY

2 She said (that) they would pay for everything.
3 She said (that) she would let me/us know as soon as possible.
4 She said (that) she had been there before.
5 She said (that) they didn't/don't understand the problem.
6 She said (that) there was/is no cheese left in the fridge.

C 1 a 2 an 3 a 4 the 5 the 6 an 7 the 8 –
9 a 10 –

25 BEN OKRI

Before you read

All the answers are possible, except **c**.

Working with the text

A 1 They are not used to wearing their best clothes. Perhaps they also know they may not be welcome if they criticise Azaro's father.
2 Because he has not visited them, or attended meetings, or made financial contributions to family events.
3 He criticises them for not helping and supporting him when he needed them.
4 The Party for the Poor and the Party of the Rich.
5 He has more money than Azaro's father, so he probably thinks the Party of the Rich will represent him better.
6 She brings in food and drinks.

B 1F *Azaro's mother has to borrow chairs from the neighbours.*
2T
3F *Azaro's parents' house doesn't have electricity.*
4F *Azaro's father is glad to say goodbye to his relations.*
5T

C 1c 2d 3e 4f 5g 6b 7h 8a

D 1 Yes, 'during his times of crisis'.
2 No. 'It was the most unfortunate change of subject.' The relation must know it will start an argument, so it is a silly thing to do.
3 No. The women go out into the passage with Azaro's mother, and talk and laugh together, while the men sit silently in the room.
4 It is getting hotter, so people are losing their tempers. Some people have had a few drinks, and perhaps are becoming too outspoken.
5 They have more money than him.
6 He is angry that the Party of the Rich gave it away to the people in order to win their votes.

F **b** is correct.

Language work

A 1d I insist *on* seeing the manager at once!
2g We succeeded *in* getting the car to start.
3e The old lady accused him *of* breaking into her flat.
4f I really object *to* people smoking during meals.
5b Why don't you apply *for* Lucy's job, when she leaves?
6a I'm sorry, but I don't agree *with* any of your ideas.
7c Liz's parents didn't approve *of* the man she wanted to marry.

B 1 After I *had had* a bath, I *went* to bed.
2 After he *had done* the shopping, he *had* a coffee.
3 I *had never visited* the area before we *came* to live here in 1999.
4 She *did not go* with Sam to the theatre because she *had already seen* the play.
5 By the time she *left* school, Susie *had learnt* five languages.
6 The police *told* us they *had already searched* most of the forest.

C 1c 2d 3e 4f 5a 6g 7b

26 ANITA DESAI

Before you read

a and **b** are correct.

Working with the text

A 1 The radio.
2 Suno's father.
3 The radio newsreader giving news of terrible disasters that have happened in the world.
4 Very angry with his father for having the radio on so loud.
5 He means he won't smash the radio on to his father's head, throw it out of the window or *do anything like that*. He won't do these things because he must be polite to his father.
6 No. Suno is exaggerating, making the situation sound much worse than it really is, to show us how difficult it is for him to study – and to make us laugh.
7 Suno's mother.
8 His uncle's.

B 1F Suno's mother spends *all day* cooking.
2F She uses plenty of *tap* water in the kitchen.
3T
4F Suno *accidentally knocks over* a glass of milk.
5T
6F The children *have no idea how* to be quiet when they come home from school.

C 1d 2f 3a 4c 5g 6i 7e 8b 9h

D 1c 2d 3f 4a 5b 6e

141

KEY

E Broom, brroom, brrroom, roars, fries, chopping, slicing, hissing, roaring, pouring, rings, clash, clatter, break, marching, hammering, clangs, uproar, sloshes, sizzles, bawl, screech, whacks.

F [*Note to teachers:* elicit from students the idea that while Suno's most obvious problem is the noise all around him, he may be using it as an excuse not to study. The stress involved in preparing for an exam and his parents' high expectations of him are the real causes of his anxiety.]

G **b** and **d** are correct.

Language work

A 1 noisiest 2 laziest 3 most annoyed 4 worst 5 quietest

B 1 hot 2 tired 3 cold 4 important/urgent 5 good/intelligent/nice/generous man

27 JOHN STEINBECK

Before you read

1 **e** is correct.
2 **c** is correct.

Working with the text

A 1 There is a strong wind, blowing sticks and sand at Kino and Juana.
   2 In a northerly direction.
   3 The wind will blow away their footprints in the sand.
   4 By the light of the stars.
   5 Their footprints will be less noticeable.
   6 a Sand is blown into the footprints by the wind.
     b Kino sweeps the footprints away, using a branch.
     c Carts and wagons drive through the ruts and cover the footprints.

B 1d 2a 3f 4c 5g 6b 7e

C 1F *The wind throws* sticks, sand and small rocks at Kino and his family.
   2F *Nobody* sees the family pass by.
   3F Juana walks *behind* Kino.
   4F Kino is afraid of being *followed by someone*.
   5T

D 1 There are no clouds; the stars are clear, in a black sky.
   2 So that no one knows they are leaving.
   3 'The music of the pearl' is Kino's joy at owning the pearl and his feeling that this is his one chance to change his life. 'The quiet melody of the family' means Kino's love for his wife and son, and his feeling of responsibility for them. He is determined to use the pearl to give his family a better future, and not let anyone take it from him.

F 1b, 2b and 3a are correct.

Language work

A 1 in 2 to 3 by 4 over 5 from, to

B 1 The girls' homework is on the table – they've just finished it.
   2 Ted's son is staying at Bob's house tonight.
   3 The fans shouted and waved excitedly as the Real Madrid team's bus arrived.
   4 I watched the postman's van drive up the hill and stop at Miss Smith's cottage.
   5 Dad's keys were in his pocket, but Amanda's were missing.
   6 Have you looked down the street? The Turners' house is for sale!
   7 The teachers' room is on the first floor – they're having a meeting there at the moment.

C 1c That's the man *who* owns the shop.
   2e Can you tell me the reason *why* that happened?
   3a That was the moment *when* I understood the truth.
   4d We stayed in a hotel *which* was very expensive.
   5b This is the town *where* I grew up.

28 KAZUO ISHIGURO

Before you read

1 [*Note to teachers:* **c** is correct, but it is better not to give students this answer. They will find it out as they work through the unit.]
2 A difficult life, most of the time. He would have to be in charge of serving all the meals, be in charge of the drinks, organise parties and dinners, supervise all the other servants in the house, employ new servants and dismiss lazy ones, and generally be responsible for the smooth running of the whole house.

Working with the text

A 1 He thinks he should keep some secrets to himself.
   2 They are rich; they have more money than most other people.
   3 He feels he has spent all his energy on doing his best work for Lord Darlington, and now he can't do the job as well as he used to.
   4 Because Stevens has started crying. The handkerchief isn't clean; it has been used.
   5 He is dead; 'he passed away'.
   6 He was a brave man who made his own decisions.
   7 Stevens thinks he himself cannot even be proud of making his own mistakes, because he simply trusted Lord Darlington and did what Lord Darlington asked him. Lord Darlington was different because he thought for himself, and any mistakes he made were his own fault.
   8 He thinks it's a great opportunity to relax, and a very happy time. 'Been happy as a lark since the day I retired.'
   9 'Put your feet up and enjoy it (retirement).'

KEY

B 1F Stevens *works* for an American, Mr Farraday./Stevens used to work for *Lord Darlington*.
2F *Stevens* gave his best to *Lord Darlington*.
3F Stevens *often* makes mistakes in his work.
4T
5T
6F The stranger *doesn't really understand* everything Stevens says.

C 1c 2d 3a 4e 5b

D 1 a He is enjoying the view of the sea.
 b He is happy to be retired.
2 Stevens doesn't want to admit he's crying, and perhaps he doesn't think the handkerchief is clean enough. He feels ashamed about crying in public. He is crying, not because he is tired, but because he has realised he was wrong to devote his entire life to serving Lord Darlington, and now he has nothing to look forward to.

E 5 [*Note to teachers:* this means that the later stages of life (including retirement) are the best parts of people's lives. This explains the title of the book.]

F **c** is correct.

Language work

B 1e 2c 3a 4f 5d 6b

C *Taking a gerund:* mind, avoid, enjoy
1 helping   2 to give   3 spending   4 to take on
5 to lend   6 bumping